Syria
The Land of Lebanon

Syria
The Land of Lebanon

by Lewis Gaston Leary

with a new introduction by
Paul Rich

WESTPHALIA PRESS
An imprint of Policy Studies Organization

Syria The Land of Lebanon

Westphalia Press
An imprint of Policy Studies Organization
1527 New Hampshire Ave., NW
Washington, D.C. 20036
dgutierrezs@ipsonet.org

ISBN-13: 978-1935907640
ISBN-10: 1935907646

Updated material and comments on this edition
can be found at the Westphalia Press website:
www.westphaliapress.org

Preface to the New Edition:
Lewis Gaston Leary in Syria

Lewis Gaston Leary (1877-1951) was a Presbyterian minister with a facility for languages and a lifelong interest in remote places. The yearn to travel brought him to Andorra and Palestine and resulted in this still useful book about Syria.

He graduated from Rutgers in 1897 and some idea of his brilliance is shown in that he took the leaving prizes in history, debate, oratory, and metaphysics. In 1900 he received the M.A. in English literature form New York University and then earned the Ph.D. from New York in Arabic and Hebrew. He taught at the American College in Beirut, a period which informs much of this volume.

His writings on the Middle East were based on years spent there and on a command of the languages. In contrast, what passes for scholarship that has been prompted by the recent wars there demonstrates that while there was plenty of straightforward advice to be had from the past, history useful before matters became so serious, there have been few takers. Most of what is offered is shallow and is without any investigation of the events over many years that have led to the current chaos.

A heavy price has been exacted for this American lack of knowledge about the Arab world. As retreat is sounded in Iraq and Afghanistan, soldiers are probably encountering snipers using hidden sites that their grandfathers used against the occupiers in the aftermath of World War I. Now we are embarking on a crash course regarding Greater Syria.

The caravan moves on. Shortly after Donald Rumsfeld resigned as Secretary of Defense in the Bush administration, I was at a Washington reception and noticed his forlorn figure in a corner of the room, completely alone with the shrimp. No doubt just a few weeks before he would have been surrounded by admirers. Now he was a pariah in an unforgiving town.

He had learned the hard way what Calvin Coolidge wrote in 1925, that "No nation ever had an army large enough to guarantee it against attack in time of peace or insure it victory in time of war." Seldom has their been a great country where statecraft been less informed by history or the results more tragic.

Paul Rich
Garfield House, Washington

SYRIA THE LAND OF LEBANON

BY

LEWIS GASTON LEARY, PH.D.

FORMERLY INSTRUCTOR IN THE AMERICAN COLLEGE, BEIRUT, SYRIA

Author of *The Real Palestine of To-day*, *Andorra, the Hidden Republic*, etc.

AFFECTIONATELY DEDICATED

TO HIM WHO FIRST TURNED MY THOUGHTS

TOWARD SYRIA

MY FORMER PRECEPTOR AND ALWAYS

LOYAL FRIEND

GEORGE L. ROBINSON

Evening in the harbor of Beirut

PREFACE

Although Syria possesses a rare natural beauty and boasts a wealth of historic and religious interest, its fame has been so overshadowed by that of the neighboring Land of Israel that most travelers are content to take the easy railway journey to Baalbek and Damascus, and know nothing of the wild mountain valleys and snow-capped summits of Lebanon or the many ancient shrines of a country whose history reaches far back of the classic days of Greece.

It is therefore with great pleasure that I accede to the request of the publishers of my "Real Palestine of To-day" and supplement the earlier work by the present companion-volume on Syria; so that, though the books may be read independently, the two together may give a complete view of the lands of the Bible.

The chapter on Palmyra is from the pen of Professor Harvey Porter, Ph.D., of the Syrian Protestant College; and for many of the hitherto unpublished photographs I am indebted to other members of the faculty of that institution. Grateful acknowledgment is also made to *The World To-day*, *The New Era*, *The Sunday School Times*, *The Newark* (N. J.) *News*, and especially to *Travel* and *Scribner's Magazine*, for permission to include material which originally appeared in these publications.

In the writing of Arabic words, my aim has been smooth reading, rather than a systematic transliteration of the numerous sounds which are not found in English. As an aid to pronunciation, it should be noted that the stress always falls upon a syllable bearing a circumflex accent.

It will be seen that this book is written from a more intimate and personal viewpoint than the volume on Palestine. I could not write otherwise of the country which was for years my own home and where to-day I have many cherished friends among both Syrians and Franks. In fact, I must write very slowly; for every now and then I lay down my pen and, with a homesick lump in my throat, dream over again the happy days in that land of wondrous beauty which I still love with all my heart.

LEWIS GASTON LEARY

Pelham Manor, N. Y.,
October 15, 1913.

CONTENTS

THE ILLUSTRATIONS

THE ILLUSTRATIONS

Maps and Plans

SYRIA
THE LAND
OF
LEBANON

Syria, The Land of Lebanon

CHAPTER I

THE WHITE MOUNTAIN

FAR off on the eastern horizon the thin haze of an October dawn gently blended into denser masses of silvery white, which rose like dream mountains above the edge of the placid azure sea. The soft, ethereal shapes did not change their outlines, however, as clouds do; and, as the steamer drew nearer to them, the rounded forms gradually took on an appearance of bulk and solidity. These were no mere piles of morning mist, but the massive shoulders of the ancient, famous, glorious range whose strange silvery tint when viewed from afar caused it long, long ago to be called *Lebanon* — the "White Mountain."

As we approached the shore, the sun rose into a sky of brighter blue than ever domed Italian seas, and great waves of color swept downward over the round white mountainsides. I have traveled since in many lands; I know the beauty of Amalfi's cliffs, the rich tints of the southern coast of Spain, the mystic alpenglow on the snow-clad peaks of Switzerland and the delicate opalescence of the Isles of Greece; but I have never seen — I never expect to see — another glory of earth which can compare with the wondrous coloring of the mountains of Lebanon.

We watched floods of red and orange sweep across the lofty summits and then brighten into crowns of mellow gold. We looked into gorges tinged with a purple so rich and deep that the color itself seemed almost a tangible thing. Nearer still we drew, and at the foot of the mountains there came into view dark forests of evergreen and broad, sloping orchards set here and there with tiny villages of shining white. Then there appeared long lines of silvery surf and yellow sand; and we skirted the northern edge of a rock-bound promontory to the crowded harbor of Beirut.

The wording of the Old Testament might lead one to infer that Lebanon is a single mountain, and the modern Syrians also familiarly refer to it as *ej-Jebel* —"The Mountain." It is not, however, an isolated peak, but an entire range, which begins at the northern border of Palestine and stretches for a hundred miles along the easternmost shore of the Mediterranean. The narrow coastal plain cannot be distinguished at a distance. Straight out of the water the thousand summits rise in ever loftier ranks up to the level profile of the central ridge, two miles above the sea.

This "goodly mountain," which dying Moses longed to see, became to Hebrew poets the consummate symbol of all that was most strong and virile, most beautiful and enduring. The springs of Lebanon, the forests of Lebanon, the glory of Lebanon — of these they dreamed and, in ecstatic eulogy or lofty spiritual hope, of these they loved to sing. "Thou art a fountain of gardens, a well of living waters, and flowing streams from Lebanon," exclaims the hero of the Song of Songs. "The smell of thy garments is like the smell of Lebanon." The bride, too, sings of her lover, "His aspect is like Lebanon, excellent as the cedars."[1] In more solemn vein, the prophets who spoke of the coming Day of Jehovah drew imperishable imagery from these northern mountains. "The desert shall rejoice, and blossom as the rose. . . . The glory of Lebanon shall be given unto it."[2] Israel "shall blossom as the lily, and cast forth his roots as Lebanon. . . . They that dwell under his shadow shall return; they shall revive as the grain, and blossom as the vine: the scent thereof shall be as the wine of Lebanon."[3] "The glory of Lebanon shall come unto thee, the fir-tree, the pine, and the box-tree together."[4]

Toward evening I strolled out to the end of the

[1] Song of Songs 4:11f, 5:15.
[2] Isaiah 35:1f.
[3] Hosea 14:5, 7.
[4] Isaiah 60:13.

cape and looked for the first time upon what those of us who have called Beirut our home may be pardoned for believing to be the loveliest prospect in all this beautiful world. From this point can be viewed eighty miles of a coast which in the time of Abraham had already seen the rise and fall of many a proud civilization. To the south is the ancient city of Sidon, thirty miles away, and the rocky point of Sarepta and, in the dim distance, the bold headland of the "Ladder of Tyre." To the north, beyond the gorges of the River of Death and the Dog River, is the River of Adonis, where the loves of heaven and earth were celebrated many centuries before there were Greeks in Greece. Still farther north, Jebail — ancient Byblos — disputes Damascus' claim to be the oldest of cities; and thirty-five miles away the view of the coast is closed by the cape which the Greeks called *Theoprosopon*, the "Face of God." The Syrians, however, have named this *Ras esh-Shukkah* or the "Split-off Point," and say that it was torn away from the mountain and thrown bodily into the sea during the great earthquake of July 9, 551, A. D. In this land of fearful cataclysms, the story is quite possible of belief.

At the west is the expanse of the "Great Sea." At the east, just back of the cape, are the great mountains. Everything along the shore of the Mediterranean is warm, almost tropical in its verdure,

View along the coast north of Beirut

Looking up the western slopes of Lebanon

and resplendent in the orient hues painted by the Syrian sun. The lower slopes of Lebanon are soft with vineyards and groves of olive, fig and mulberry. Above the green orchards and white villages are dark pine forests, and somber gorges cut deep between smooth, swelling moorlands. Higher still the desolate, lonely slopes are quite bare of vegetation; yet, in the clear atmosphere, they seem as soft as if they were overlaid with bright velvets and shimmering silks. Last of all, the eye is drawn up to the summits of Kencisch and Sunnin, tinged with orange and purple in the summer sunset, and in winter covered with vast sheets of snow.

From the tropics to the chill barrenness of the arctics — it is all comprehended in one glorious panorama. What an Arabic poet wróte of yonder towering Sunnin is true of the whole range —

> " He bears winter upon his head,
> Spring upon his shoulders,
> Autumn in his bosom,
> While summer lies slumbering at his feet."

But Lebanon is more than a splendid spectacle. There would be no Syria, no fertile mother of the olive and orange, no land of the long martial history, no tale of ancient culture or modern enterprise, save for the Mountain, whose lofty peaks break the rain-clouds borne hither by the west winds and drop their precious moisture on the thirsty soil below.

CHAPTER II

THE LEFT-HAND LAND

THE Arab geographer always faces towards the east. So the southernmost portion of the Arabian peninsula is to him the *Yemen* or "Right," and this northern district of ours is called *esh-Shâm* or the "Left-hand Land." The name *Surîya* or "Syria," an ancient corruption of "Assyria," is also, however, frequently employed, especially by the Turks.

As this territory is not a modern political unit, its limits are variously defined, both by natives and foreigners. The whole country between Asia Minor and Egypt is often called Syria, and its inhabitants, who have the same language and customs and are of practically the same — very mixed — blood, are known as Syrians. But from the historical viewpoint it is perhaps more exact to distinguish between Palestine and Syria, and confine the latter name to the territory which lies to the north of the Hebrew boundary-town of Dan.

Syria then, as we shall use the word, extends from the southern slopes of Mount Hermon to the Bay of Alexandretta, a distance of about two hundred and fifty miles. It is a long, narrow country. At the west is the Mediterranean; at the east is the Syrian Desert; within these boundaries, the width is never more than fifty miles.

The wealth and power of Syria have always been found in its southern half — the country of Lebanon. Here the mountains are divided into two parallel ranges by the long valley which the Greeks called "Hollow Syria." Between this valley and the Mediterranean is Lebanon; between the valley and the desert is the twin range of Anti-Lebanon.[1] The western mountains rise gradually toward their northern end, where they attain an elevation of over 11,000 feet. The eastern chain, however, reaches its culmination in its southernmost peak, Mount Hermon, which is 9,000 feet above the sea. On the coastal plain beside Lebanon lie the ancient cities of Tyre, Sidon and Byblos and the modern ports of Beirut and Tripoli. On a peninsula of fertility watered by the streams of Anti-Lebanon, Damascus stands between the mountains and the desert. The rest of Syria is made up of lofty summits, rocky gorges resounding with the tumult of cave-born torrents, high wind-swept pasture lands and broad, fertile valleys slanting up between the mountains.

The lovelorn Syrian does not sing dolefully of a sweetheart who "lies over the ocean." To him the typical barrier is not the sea. *Beni ubenik ej-jebel*

1 See map, page 62, and cross-section, page 64.

runs the plaintive lament—"Between me and thee is the mountain." The country is more crowded with towering peaks than Palestine or Greece, but it is more fertile than either. No other region of equal size has such a variety of vegetable life; no other land is more healthful; and to those of us who have lived in the shadow of Lebanon, none is more beautiful.

Syria, as we have defined it, includes one entire *vilâyet*, or province, of the Turkish Empire and parts of three others. Its extreme northern portion is included in the great Vilayet of Aleppo, which stretches far across the desert to Mesopotamia. Anti-Lebanon and most of Hollow Syria lie within the Vilayet of *esh-Shâm* or "Syria." This important province, whose capital is Damascus, takes in all the arable land east of the Jordan as far as the southern end of the Dead Sea. The independent *Mutesarrifîyet*, or sub-province, of Lebanon is practically co-extensive with this range, but touches the Mediterranean only for a few miles and has no seaport. Almost the entire coast belongs to the Vilayet of Beirut, which reaches from Mount Akra, a hundred and fifty miles north of the provincial capital, to within sight of the harbor of Jaffa and includes nearly all of Palestine west of the Jordan River.

In the absence of any census, we can hardly do more than guess at the population of Syria. It is probably above two million. The Turkish residents are for the most part government officials, and there are few Jews outside of Beirut and Damascus. The mass of the inhabitants are descendants of the Syrians, or Arameans, of Biblical times; but the native blood has been mixed with that of many other races. It is scarcely correct to call these people "Arabs," except in the sense that they are an Arabic-speaking race. In countenance, as well as customs, they differ considerably from their less civilized cousins who roam the neighboring deserts.

The ecclesiastical bodies of Syria are numerous, jealous and extremely fanatical. In striking contrast to the awkward reticence of the West regarding religious matters, every Syrian not only counts himself an adherent of the faith into which he was born, but he thrusts that fact upon your attention and, on the slightest provocation, is ready to fight for his belief. A man's ancestors, descendants and home may be cursed with all the wealth of Oriental vituperation, and he will probably accept this as a mere emphatic conversational embellishment. But let the single word *dinak!* "thy religion!" be spoken with a curseful intonation to a follower of a different faith, and the spirit of murder is let loose.

Islam is, of course, the official religion of the government; but in the southern half of the country the majority of the inhabitants are Christians. The most powerful church is the Greek Orthodox; next in importance come the Maronites and Greek Catholics, who render allegiance to the Pope of Rome. Nearly a dozen other sects, exclusive of the Protestants, are actively working and hating and scheming in Syria. Many of the members of these Oriental churches are sincere and devout; but, on the whole, the organized Christianity of Syria, like that of neighboring Palestine,[2] has been so inextricably entangled with political ambitions, sectarian jealousy and civil warfare that its moral and religious teachings are in danger of being completely neglected.

Syrian Mohammedanism is also divided against itself, though not to such a hazardous degree as is Syrian Christianity. Many villages in northern Lebanon are occupied by adherents of the schismatic Shiite sect. These Metawileh, as they are called, bear an unenviable reputation for their ignorance, dishonesty, brutality and, what is very unusual in Syria, their lack of hospitality. They will refuse accommodations to a traveler and are accustomed to break the earthenware drinking-jug which has been defiled by the touch of a stranger. Still farther north there survive a few settlements of the Ismailians, who during the Middle Ages were known as the *Assassins* — literally, "hashish-smokers." Their character is sufficiently indicated by the fact that the only thing they gave the Western world was the word "assassin."

[2] See further the author's *The Real Palestine of To-day*, chapter III.

In the mountains which bear their name are a hundred thousand Nusairiyeh, who migrated hither many centuries ago from Mesopotamia and still hold to a strange, mystic nature-worship. Traces of the vile phallic cults of ancient Syria are also found among the wilder regions of the north.

The sixty thousand Druses of central and southern Lebanon are frequently confused with the Moslems by careless writers; on the other hand they are sometimes referred to as a Christian sect. As a matter of fact, they are neither. Although this faith originated among followers of Islam, the early Druses suffered many persecutions at the hands of the Moslems, who classed them as "infidels," while their feuds with the Christian populace of Lebanon have led to some of the most cruel and bitter struggles of modern times.

In the eleventh century an insane ruler of Egypt named Hakim Biamrillah declared himself to be the *Imâm*, or incarnation of the Deity, and his preposterous claims found an enthusiastic prophet in a Persian resident of Cairo called ed-Durazy, from whom is derived the familiar name "Druse." The adherents of this sect, however, call themselves *Muwahhidîn*, or "Unitarians." Such was the wrath of the Egyptian Moslems at el-Durazy's preaching that he was forced to flee to the mountains of Syria, where the new faith spread rapidly among the inhabitants of Hermon and southern Lebanon. Shortly after ed-Durazy's flight the caliph Hakim mysteriously disappeared. Doubtless he was assassinated; but the Druses believe that he is miraculously concealed until the appointed day of his final revelation as the victorious *Mahdi*.

The peculiar doctrines of the Druses were systematized by a companion of the prophet's exile, Hamzeh ibn Ahmed, since known as the "Guide." The tenets of this faith are still, however, only partly understood by Western scholars; for its most important beliefs are kept in great secrecy, none of the women and only a very small proportion of the men are initiated into its esoteric teachings, converts to other faiths are practically unknown, and the Druses hold that, in conversation with a Moslem or a Christian, it is permissible for them to pretend acquiescence in the other's statements.

Their extreme emphasis on the unity of God, whom they divest of all attributes, goes even beyond that of Mohammedanism. Yet this is accompanied by a belief in the divine self-revelation through a succession of incarnations which began with Adam and ended with the Caliph Hakim and included Jesus and Mohammed. They also hold the doctrine of transmigration of souls and think that many of them will be reincarnated in the heart of China, where, according to their strange tradition, there are multitudes of Chinese Druses. They do not practice the Moslem virtues of prayer, fasting, formal almsgiving and the pilgrimage to Mecca; but the few initiates rigorously abstain from both wine and tobacco.

Probably all that most Druses know about their religion is that they are Druses. Yet their feeling of separation from the other inhabitants of the country, which amounts to a sense of racial difference, has made them the most proud and independent — not to say ungovernable — class in the Turkish Empire. The faces of the Druse men are the handsomest and haughtiest in Syria, and their forms are tall and stalwart. They are a brave, intellectual, courteous, hospitable people; they treat their wives far better than do the Moslems, and in time of war they never massacre women. Some of the Druse emirs whom I have met are refined, correctly dressed, well-educated gentlemen who are as much at home on the boulevards of Paris as they are among their own mountains. Yet anything more than a superficial acquaintance with them is prevented by the suave hypocrisy which their religion inculcates; their otherwise admirable courage is marred by heartless cruelty and a relentless carrying out of the ancient law of blood for blood; and the splendid organization with which they meet the aggressions of an alien enemy is weakened by their interminable intertribal feuds. The history of the great Druse families of Lebanon is stained by many an awful record of treachery, fratricide and massacre.

In the summer of 1860, twenty years of intermittent altercations between the Druses and Maronites culminated in an outbreak of fearful religious warfare. The Druses were perhaps no braver than their opponents; but they showed better discipline, had more able leaders and, from the beginning, were encouraged by the support of the Moslem government. So the war soon developed into a mere succession of massacres of the unfortunate Maronites. Turkish officials connived at these outrages, and Turkish regiments, presumably sent to restore order in the troubled districts, either disarmed the Christians and then turned them over to be dealt with by their enemies, or else themselves added to the horrors of the slaughter by killing even the women whom the Druses had spared. Maronite monasteries were sacked and their monks put to death with barbarous tortures, a hundred villages were burned, and multitudes of unarmed peasants who had sought protection in the courtyards of government buildings were allowed to be shot down by their relentless enemies. It will never be known just how many Christians were slain during that awful summer. Seven thousand are said to have perished in Damascus alone; and some conception of the vast number of survivors who were left homeless and destitute is gained when we learn that the Anglo-American Relief Committee of Beirut had upon its lists the names of twenty-seven thousand refugees.

The Christian nations were shocked into activity by the terrible tidings from Syria. Fifty European warships soon reached the harbor of Beirut, and an army of ten thousand French soldiers was landed. Just in time to avoid foreign intervention, however, the sultan sent two of his own regiments from Constantinople to quell the disturbance, and shortly afterwards the grand vizier himself came to Syria with additional troops. These soldiers were but a handful in comparison with the Druse army or even the Turkish regiments which had been assisting in the slaughter; but when the mysterious, unwritten messages go forth from Constantinople commanding that a massacre shall be stopped — or shall be begun — they are understood at once in the most inaccessible mountain villages of the empire.

As soon as order was restored, the conscription, from which holy Damascus had been exempt since the days of Mohammed, was strictly enforced as a punitive measure; and over twenty thousand Damascene Moslems were sent in chains to the coast, whence they were transported to regiments in distant provinces of Turkey. Furthermore, a levy of a million dollars was laid upon the city, and its governor and a hundred prominent Moslem residents were hanged for their share in the massacres, as were also a few officials in other parts of the country. Not a single Druse, however, was executed for partaking in the awful slaughter.

The European powers now insisted that there should never be another Moslem ruler over the Christians of Lebanon, and such pressure was brought to bear upon the Turkish government that the district was made a practically independent province. Its governor must be, like the Maronites, a Latin Christian, although, in justice to the Druse population, he may not be an inhabitant of Syria. His appointment is subject to the approval of the six great powers and he cannot be removed without the consent of their ambassadors at Constantinople. The province pays no taxes to the imperial government, nor may Turkish troops be stationed within its boundaries except under certain stringent restrictions. Lebanon has its own army of volunteer militia; and the free, independent bearing of these mountaineers is in striking contrast to that of the underpaid, underfed and poorly clothed conscripts of the regular army.

The rulers appointed under the new régime have not all been equally capable and honest. Some have understood the language of *bakhsheesh* as well as their Turkish predecessors. The commercial growth of the province has also been hampered by the lack of a seaport. Yet since 1861 the mountaineers, Druses and Maronites alike, have enjoyed an unprecedented quiet and an increasing material prosperity. The old feudal wars have ceased, the tyrannical political power of the Maronite hierarchy

A guard of Lebanon soldiers

The village of Deir El-Kamr, where no Druse dare dwell

is greatly diminished, education is rapidly advancing and the valuation of property in the Lebanon district has greatly advanced. In the words of Lord Dufferin, who was a member of the international commission which framed the new plan of government, "until the present day the Lebanon has been the most peaceful, the most contented and the most prosperous province of the Ottoman Dominion."

Yet the cruel past has not entirely sunk into oblivion. The Maronite village of Deir el-Kamr, for instance, has still one mosque; but no Moslem dwells there, nor dare a Druse pass through this neighborhood where the massacre of unarmed Christians lasted until more than two thousand corpses lay within the enclosure of the government-house. On the other hand, there are Druse hamlets where no Maronite would trust himself. Ten years ago, when Beirut was in one of its periodic tumults, five thousand Lebanon soldiers, stalwart, brave and well-armed, encamped just outside the city limits, waiting for one more anti-Christian outbreak — which fortunately did not come — as an excuse for wiping out the Moslem population. Looking across a deep gorge of Lebanon, I once saw a file of Turkish soldiers laboriously making their way up the steep mountainside. They were seeking a murderer, so I was told, but a murderer of no common mettle; for from his inaccessible retreat among the cliffs he had sent to the government of Beirut a bold acknowledgment of his crimes, accompanied by the threat that whenever in the future a Christian should be assassinated in that city he would immediately descend to the coast and take the life of a Moslem in exchange.

On a stormy winter night I sat by the charcoal fire in a Maronite hut high up among the mountains, and heard read from a grimy, much-thumbed manuscript a long poem which described the brave part played by that village in the struggles of fifty years ago. The sonorous Arabic sentences had almost an Homeric ring. Like the list of Grecian ships sounded the rhythmic roll of the local heroes of half a century gone by. And as the dull light of the fire shone on the circle of dark, bearded mountaineers, the grim lines of their faces showed that the valor of the village had not weakened with the passing years, nor had the wrongs of the village fathers been forgot.

To the traveler, bewildered by strange customs and by peculiar ways of doing familiar things, this seems indeed a "Left-hand Land." The Syrian holds a loose sheet of paper in his palm and writes from right to left. Yet numbers are written, like ours, from left to right. In beckoning, the fingers are turned downward. To nod "No" the head is jerked upward, and added emphasis is sometimes given by a sharp cluck of the tongue. The carpenter draws his saw toward him on the cutting stroke. The oarsman likes to stand up and face the bow of his boat. When digging, one man holds the handle of the shovel while two others do most of the work by pulling it with ropes. Except in cities which have felt European influence, it is the men who wear skirts or flowing bloomers, and the women who wear trousers. Keys are put into the locks upside down. In entering a house, the hat is kept on the head, but the shoes are removed.

Grown men greet one another in public with embraces and kisses. You see them walking along hand in hand, or smelling little nosegays. Yet these acts are not necessarily indicative of effeminacy. For all you know, these same fellows may occupy their leisure moments with highway robbery. The slightest difference of opinion gives rise to excited vituperation and offensive gesticulation; but a blow is seldom given. When a Syrian does smite, he employs no halfway measures: he smites to kill. I only once saw a blow struck in anger: then a club four inches thick was, without warning, brought down with full force upon the head of an unfortunate boatman.

In this topsy-turvy land, parents take the name of their first-born son, and use it even in signing legal papers. The gate-keeper at the American College, for instance, was never called anything but Abu Mohammed, "the Father of Mohammed." When a son is despaired of, the public humiliation is sometimes avoided by inventing one. It is quite possible that Abu Zeki or Abu Saïd has no children at all.

The daughters of the family are often called after jewels or flowers or constellations; yet, except in Protestant families, the birth of a girl is not an occasion for rejoicing. One father insisted on christening an unwelcome girl baby Balash, which might be translated "Nothing doing!" Another parent, who already had six daughters, was so disgusted at the advent of a seventh that he named her Bikeffeh, "Enough!" A Maronite proverb says, "The threshold mourns forty days when a girl is born." Nevertheless the lot of the Christian woman, even in communities where Christianity means hardly more than a political organization, is usually far better than that of her Moslem sisters.

Surnames are very indefinite and shifting matters. If Musa has a son named Jurjus, the boy will naturally be known as Jurjus Musa. But the father will, of course, change his own name to Abu Jurjus. Many surnames are taken from occupations. Haddad or "Smith" is here, as in every country, one of the most common. Others are derived from localities. Hanna Shweiri is "John from Shweir," and Suleiman Beiruti is "Beirut Solomon." Real family or clan names, however, are not uncommon, especially among the aristocracy.

As a man becomes more prosperous he will often

drop his commonplace appellation in favor of a more dignified one, which perhaps revives an ancient but long neglected designation of his family. This easy putting on and off of names sometimes leads to considerable confusion. I once asked all over a mountain village for the house of a friend whom I had known in Beirut, and met with the most positive assurances that no such person lived there. Fortunately I happened to remember that my friend's father was a baker. "John Baker! Oh, yes, everybody in town knows *him!* But that other fellow you've been asking about — we never heard of him."

The mountain boys, especially, used often to take new surnames when they came to college. Sometimes they afterward exchanged these for still better ones. So a facetious professor greeted a returning student with "Well, Eliya, what is your name *this* year?" An exasperated inquirer, who had vainly tried to pin down a certain youth to a satisfactory statement of his chosen titles, finally exclaimed, "Now, tell me, what *is* your name?" Then came the maddeningly irritating answer which so frequently tempts the Occidental to commit homicide, "As you like, sir!" Another young man, who had narrowly escaped expulsion for his various misdeeds, decided to turn over a new leaf; so he came back to the college the next autumn with a different name — and made it good. The Syrian understands better than do we the full content of the divine promise of "a new name."[3]

At first this seems a land of inexplicable contrasts. I could write of its ravaging pestilences so that one would find it hard to believe that Syria is notable for its healthfulness. I could record fearful massacres until the reader would think me foolishly daring for never carrying a weapon during all my travels. I could — quite truthfully — tell how a Syrian landscape lacks so many of the old familiar aspects of our home scenes, and give no hint of the glorious panoramas of this fertile, well-watered, bright-colored land — where the mountains sit with their feet in the Great Sea and their heads among the glorious clouds, while mantles of shimmering silver fall above their richly tinted garments.

As is the land, so are its people; not easy to understand and justly appraise. They are cruel and cunning and prefer to destroy an enemy by a sudden rush of overwhelming odds rather than to meet him in equal combat. Yes, this is true of many of them; yet they have a childlike delight in sweet scents, bright colors, beautiful flowers and simple games. Although they may live in poverty and squalor, they are very frugal and temperate. They are ignorant; but when the opportunity comes they study with a pathetic earnestness and an unrivaled quickness. At half-past three of cold winter morn-

[3] Rev. 2:17, etc.

ings I used to hear a servant going the rounds of my dormitory to waken the young men, at their own request, so that they might spend four hours before breakfast at their books. Some of those same indefatigable students have since led their classes in great American and European universities.

It is true that the Syrians nurse vengeful feuds for generation after generation. That is partly because family ties are so wonderfully strong among them. "I and my brother against my cousin; I and my cousin against my neighbor," runs the proverb. When two brothers are in the same class at school or college, they seldom have other chums, but insist upon sitting side by side in the classroom, and during their free hours they wander about the campus with arms around each other's shoulders. If an elder brother goes away to make his fortune in some distant country, he never forgets the loved ones at home; but year after year the remittances will come, until all the younger children have been educated or have been brought across the sea to share in the opportunities of the new land of promise. A trusted American missionary had at one time in his possession no less than five thousand dollars which had been sent from America for the parents and younger children of a single mountain village.

The ambition of the Syrian is as boundless as his daring, and his courageous persistence is a buttress to his splendid capacity for both business and scholarship. The son of any laboring man may, for all one knows, become a high Egyptian official, a wealthy merchant of the Argentine, a French poet or the pastor of an American church. The "Arab" dragoman of your tourist party may be the proud father of a boy whose learned works in choicest English you hope sometime to read, or whose surgical skill may be called upon to carry you through a critical operation. These are not fanciful possibilities. I have particular names in mind as I write; and the tale of the bravely endured hardships of some of these sons of Syria who have made good in many a far-off land would match the romantic story of the early struggles of Garfield or Lincoln.

The hospitality of the Syrians is no mere form or pretense, but a sincere, winsome joy in ministering to the poor and the stranger. Their courtesy is fortified by an invincible tact and a very keen knowledge of human nature. Their speech, the strange guttural Arabic which sounds so uncouth to the passing stranger, is one of the most beautiful, expressive and widespread of languages, and has a wealth of fascinating literature. Their religious fanaticism is grounded in an intense, unshakable belief in the fact and the necessity of a divine revelation; and he who in the heat of a ferocious bigotry will kill his neighbor is willing, if need be, to die himself for the faith, whether it be in open warfare or by the tortures of a slow martyrdom.

The native ideals of truthfulness and business honor are not, to be frank, those of Anglo-Saxon nations. It is not considered very insulting to call a Syrian a liar. But even in the Western business world all is not truth and uprightness, and these men and women have an excuse which we have not. For centuries their land has been ruled by a government based upon untruth and injustice, and very often the only protection for life or property lay in evasion and deceit. The wonder is that, in spite of all, there are still so many Syrians who would swear to their own hurt and change not, and who boldly urge upon their people the eradication of what is perhaps their greatest racial shortcoming.

In brief, with all his faults, which we of the West are apt to over-emphasize because they are not the same as our faults, the Syrian is frugal, temperate, ambitious, adaptable, intellectually brilliant, capable of infinite self-sacrifice for any great end, essentially religious, generously hospitable, courteous in social intercourse and, to his loved ones, extremely affectionate and faithful.

When to these admirable racial traits is added a sincere acceptance of the moral teachings of religion, then, whatever his creed, the Syrian makes a friend to be cherished very close to your heart.

CHAPTER III

THE CITY OF SATURN

"AND behold, I am now in Beirut." Thus wrote Prince Rib-addi to his royal master, Pharaoh Amenhotep, thirty-three centuries ago; and when the Tell el-Amarna Letters were sent from Syria to Egypt, about 1400 B. C., Beirut had long been one of the chief commercial cities of the eastern Mediterranean. According to a Greek tradition, it was founded in the Golden Age by the Titan Kronos, or Saturn, the father of Zeus. The tutelary deity of the seaport, however, was Poseidon (Neptune), another son of Saturn, who is represented on its coins driving his sea-horses, or standing on the prow of a ship with his trident in one hand and a dolphin in the other.

The authentic history of the city begins with the records of its conquerors. Rameses II. of Egypt and Sennacherib of Assyria commemorated their successful Syrian campaigns by inscriptions still existing on the cliffs of the Dog River, just north of Beirut. Centuries later, Alexander the Great marched his conquering army through the city, Pompey added it to the Roman Em-

The Bay of Beirut and Mount Sunnin

Among the pine groves of the Cape of Beirut

pire, and Augustus visited here his son-in-law, the local governor. It was in Beirut that Herod the Great appeared as the accuser of his two sons, who were thereupon convicted of conspiracy and put to death by strangling. Vespasian passed through its streets in triumphal progress on his way to assume the imperial crown, and in its immense amphitheater Titus celebrated his capture of Jerusalem by a magnificent series of shows and gladiatorial contests. During the First Crusade, Baldwin, Count of Flanders and ruler of the Latin Kingdom of Jerusalem, wrested the city from the Moslems after a long siege and put its inhabitants to the sword. Seventy years later, the greatest of all Saracen leaders, Saladin, recaptured the city from the Christians. The names of the mighty warriors who since then have fought for the possession of this old, old seaport are less familiar to Western readers; yet few cities have had for so many centuries such intimate association with the most renowned characters of history. There is a local tradition that Christ Himself visited Beirut on the occasion of His journey "into the borders of Tyre and Sidon," and during the Middle Ages there was exhibited here a miracle-working picture of Him, which was said to have been painted by Nicodemus the Pharisee.

The inner harbor, still known as *Mar Jurjus* or "St. George," is associated with what is perhaps the oldest of all myths. This took on varying forms during the millenniums of its progress westward from the Euphrates to the Atlantic. We find it first in the Babylonian Creation Epic, which tells of the destruction of the chaos-monster by the solar deity, Marduk. When the Greeks took over the ancient Asiatic mythology, it was Perseus, child of the sun-god, who slew the dragon at Jaffa and released the beautiful Andromeda. In the sixth century A. D., the exploit was transferred to St. George, whose victory over the sea-monster was perhaps an unconscious parable of the overthrow of heathenism by Christianity.

St. George appears to have been a real person, who suffered martyrdom about the year 300, possibly at Lydda in Palestine, where his tomb is still shown. Singularly enough, this Syrian Christian has not only been the patron saint of England since Richard Cœur de Lion came to the Holy Land on the Third Crusade, but is also a very popular hero of the Moslems.

The historic character had, of course, nothing to do with any dragon, and it was only many centuries after his death that he became identified with the hero of the ancient Semitic myth, under its Perseus form. A mighty monster, so the story runs, had long terrified the district of Beirut, and was prevented from destroying the city only by receiving the annual sacrifice of a beautiful virgin. One year the fateful lot fell upon the daughter of the governor. When the poor girl was taken to the appointed place, she knelt in prayer and besought God to send her a deliverer. Whereupon St. George appeared in shining armor and, after a tremendous battle, slew the monster, delivered the maiden, and freed the city from its long reign of terror. Whether, like his prototype Perseus, he married the rescued virgin, the story does not relate. We are told, however, that the grateful father built a church in honor of the valiant champion and also instituted a yearly feast in commemoration of his daughter's deliverance. During the Middle Ages, this was celebrated by Christians and Moslems alike. Beside the Dog River can still be seen the ruins of an ancient church and a mosque, both of which marked the supposed locality of the contest; and here also is a very old well, into which the body of the slain dragon is said to have been thrown.

The word *Beirût* is doubtless derived from the ancient Semitic place-name *Beeroth*,[1] which means, "wells," and throughout the Arab world such a designation immediately calls up a picture of fertile prosperity. The triangular cape on whose northern shore the city is situated projects from the foot of Lebanon five miles into the Mediterranean and has an area of about sixteen square miles. This level broadening of the coastal plain appears in striking contrast to the country just north and south of it,

1 Cf. Deut. 10:6, Josh. 9:17.

yards up these steep, slippery shafts. One day, while walking along the top of the cliff, I came upon the upper end of a natural chimney whose formation appeared so unusually regular that I became curious to see what it might lead to. So I slid down twelve or fifteen feet and dropped into the ashes of a recent fire which had been built in the center of a cozy little cave high above the water. The rocky point of the cape, honeycombed with dark passages and secret hiding-places, is a favorite resort of smugglers, especially on moonless nights; and in the bazaars of the city you can buy many articles which have not been submitted to the extortions of the Turkish customhouse. While I was a resident of Beirut, the "king of the smugglers," who lived near me, killed three revenue officers who were interfering with his illicit trade. Bribery and intimidation, however, soon removed all danger of prosecution for his various crimes; and a few days later I saw him driving defiantly along the Shore Road in his elegant carriage.

Beirut has suffered so severely from earthquakes, as well as from besieging armies, that there remain no traces of very old buildings except some columns of reddish Egyptian granite. Only a few of these can now be seen above ground or lying under water at the bottom of the harbor, where doubtless they were rolled by earthquake shocks; but from the frequency with which they appear whenever excavations are made, there must be a multitude of them scattered all over the site of the ancient city.

Among the mountains just back of the cape are the ruins of a Roman aqueduct, which supplied the city from a spring in the valley of the Beirut River, six miles away. The ravine was bridged by a series of six arches, arranged in four tiers. The lowest of these had two spans; the highest had twenty-five, and rose a hundred and sixty feet above the river-bed. On the west bank, the water was carried through a tunnel cut in the solid rock of the mountainside. This opening is now filled with fallen stones, and of the aqueduct itself there remain only a few broken arches at the eastern end; yet the massive ruin, rising high above the river amid these desolate, lonely surroundings, still suggests the wealth and enterprise of the centuries long gone by.

During the last forty years Beirut has been abundantly provided with water piped from the Dog River by an English company. So pure is this supply that since its use became common the city has not known a single outbreak of cholera or plague, though the surrounding country has often been devastated by these diseases. One memorable year we watched a fearful epidemic creep up the coast toward us, curve inland round the edge of the district supplied with Dog River water, and then sweep back again to the seashore and continue its terrible journey northward.

The Dog River was in ancient times known as the

Lycus or "Wolf" River. It is said to have received its present name from a marvelous statue of a dog set above the cliffs, which opened its stone mouth and barked lustily at the approach of a hostile ship. Indeed, to this very day a vivid imagination can discern the likeness of a huge mastiff in a certain boulder, now submerged in the center of the stream.

The pass up its rocky gorge has been trod by many a great army. The well-preserved bridge which now spans the stream was built by the sultan Selim four hundred years ago; but a Latin inscription on the cliff indicates that a military road was constructed here by Marcus Aurelius as early as the second century, and on the sheer rocks at the left bank of the river are cut panels whose records far antedate the days of Roman supremacy. Ashur-nasir-pal, Shalmaneser, Tiglath-pileser, Sennacherib, Esarhaddon, Rameses — such are the strange sounding names given to the forms in bas-relief which still lift above the rushing stream the scepters of their long-vanished power. The boastings of Greek and Arabic conquerors are also found along this path of ancient armies and — what seems in such surroundings a weak anti-climax — upon a panel which originally bore one of the Egyptian inscriptions now appears the record of the French expedition of 1860.

Four miles from the mouth of the Dog River, its principal tributary bursts from a cave which extends far into the heart of Lebanon. Within this are found stalactites of every shape and color, natural columns as large and almost as symmetrical as those of the Parthenon, enormous cathedral-like chambers, labyrinthine passages without number, deep icy pools, and cascades whose dull thunder reverberates through the dark depths of the mountain. With the aid of portable rafts, adventurous explorers have penetrated this wonderful cavern for nearly a mile; but at that distance there was no diminution of the volume of the stream or any other indication that they had come at all near to the source of the mysterious underground river. The light of their torches but dimly revealed the roaring torrent ceaselessly speeding out from dark, distant channels like those

> "Where Alph, the sacred river, ran
> Through caverns measureless to man
> Down to a sunless sea."

Although the Bay of Beirut opens to the Mediterranean at an obtuse angle, it is so well protected from storms by the long cape that it provides the safest anchorage between Port Saïd and Smyrna. I remember only one tempest which blew so strongly that anchors could not hold and steamers had to leave the port for the open sea. The harbor is crowded with shipping of all sizes and shapes, from the little coastwise barks and the queer, low Egyptian boats with their one triangular sail to the great transatlantic liners which bring multitudes of tourists on cruises to the Holy Land. About four thousand merchant vessels clear the port annually. Since the dawn of history, Damascus has sent its exports hither by the ancient caravan road. For the past eighteen years there has been a railway across the mountains, and its recently completed branch to Aleppo will doubtless attract more and more of the trade of northern Syria.

The exports from Beirut amount each year to over $4,000,000. About one-third of this value is made up of raw silk; other important commodities are olive oil, licorice and fruit. The character of the chief imports is determined by the fact that the mountains are almost denuded of large forest trees. Immense quantities of timber, metal girders, firewood and petroleum must therefore be brought from abroad. The dependence of Syria upon other countries for the materials used in modern construction was illustrated in the building of the American Girls' School in Beirut. The lumber came from Maine, the doors and windows from Massachusetts, the desks and chairs from New York, the clay tiles from France, the zinc roof of the cupola from England, and the glass from Austria.

The cream-colored sandstone for this and a multitude of other structures was, however, quarried near Beirut. The stone makes a fine building material,

Bridge over the Dog River built by Sultan Selim

Procession in the Serai Square of Beirut in celebration of the granting of a constitution to the Turkish Empire in 1909

as it is easily worked, attractive in appearance and very durable. But unfortunately it is at first quite porous, and newly-erected houses are dangerously damp until the rains of two or three winters have, on their way through the walls, first dissolved a certain amount of the stone and then deposited it in the interstices. So the Syrian proverb says, "When you build a house, rent it the first year to your enemy, the second year to your friend, and the third year move into it yourself."

The traveler who journeys to Beirut from the west is naturally impressed by its scenes of Oriental life; but to one who has come hither from Lebanon or Damascus or even from Jerusalem, it seems almost a European city. Here is a French gas company, an English waterworks, a German hospital and an American college; here are post and telegraph offices, a harbor filled with shipping, and the terminus of a busy railway system. Four lines of electric tram-cars furnish quick transportation through the main streets to the attractive suburbs, and many of the wealthier residents possess automobiles. A score of printing-presses are at work and daily newspapers are sold by shouting newsboys. There are a dozen good hotels; and well-equipped stores, run on European lines, are rapidly crowding out the tiny shops of the typical Oriental merchant. Gaudy billboards extol the virtues of French cosmetics, English insurance companies and American sewing machines, phonographs and shoes, or announce the subjects of the moving-picture dramas for the coming week. Carriages throng the principal thoroughfares, the better class of citizens wear European costumes, and no passenger-steamship drops anchor in the harbor without being met by the red-shirted boatmen and suave interpreters of the enterprising tourist-agencies.

To the casual visitor, Beirut seems therefore a very peaceable, matter-of-fact place. He does not experience the feeling of half-confessed uneasiness which marked his strolls through the native quarters of other Oriental cities. Yet the busy every-day life of the seaport moves upon the thin crust of a seething volcano of hate, which all too often breaks out into murderous rage.

The Moslem inhabitants are, of course, backed by all the power of the government, legal and illegal; but they are much inferior in numbers and in wealth to the Christian population. Religious jealousy is therefore never far from the boiling-point. Any insult or violence offered by an adherent of the one faith to a believer in the other is the signal for a long series of reprisals and counter-reprisals, and there is always the possibility that these may culminate in general rioting and massacre.

The morning I first landed in Beirut, the Christian watchman of the American Press was found almost literally cut in pieces. The assassin was absolutely identified by the print of his bare foot in a mass of soft mortar; but, being a Moslem, the authorities quickly released him and, without any evidence whatever, arrested a near relative of the dead man. The poor fellow had a perfect alibi, yet he was kept in prison until the family signified their willingness to have the police department refrain from any further investigation of the murder. This is a favorite method of procedure when a Moslem is guilty of a crime against a Christian.

It used to be a rare week that we heard of no assassinations, and a rarer year that knew no general rioting. One winter there was a murder each night for six weeks, Christians and Moslems being killed alternately. So regular was the succession of reprisals that a friend whom I had invited to make an evening visit with me postponed the trip on the ground that "this is the night for a Christian to be killed." Frequent rumors would reach us of impending invasions of the Christian Quarter by Moslem mobs, and more than once the portentous war-cry of *Din! Din Mohammed!*—"The Faith! The Faith of Mohammed!"— rang in the ears of the terrified Christians. The morning I ended my residence in Beirut it was a prominent Moslem who was assassinated at the door of his own home. A few days afterwards, murderous mobs swept through the city chanting, "Oh, how sweet; oh, how joyful to cut the Christians' throats!" The empty cartridges picked up after the slaughter were of the make imported exclusively for the use of the Turkish soldiers at the government barracks.

The undying religious hatred and frequent violence do not, however, endanger the lives of European or American residents, and probably never will do so unless some insane mob should get quite beyond the control of its leaders. Islam has learned the power of foreign warships. It should also be added that the native Protestants are hardly ever molested, save by accident, during these internecine conflicts; for the Moslems realize that this portion of the population never takes any part in religious strife. Even in the terrible summer of 1860, when all Syria was drenched with blood, only nine Protestants were killed.

During the past few months there has developed a new and unexpected phase of Beirut strife. Since the revolution of the Young Turks, a vigorous demand for political righteousness and even-handed justice has, in spite of all set-backs, been growing steadily among every race and faith of the empire. In Syria the new ideals and hopes found expression in the organization of a " Committee of Reform," which demanded such elemental rights as the appointment of an Arabic-speaking governor of Beirut and the use of the vernacular in the courts of justice. Up to the present time, the governor has always been a Turk, and Turkish judges have understood the language of bribery better than the Arabic pleas of poor men who appeared before them.

Last spring the differences between the people of Beirut and the government became so acute that the city was put under martial law by the pasha, who also issued a proclamation dissolving the local branch of the Reform Committee and forbidding further gatherings of the citizens or discussion in the public press. Every newspaper of the city protested against these despotic acts by printing an issue which was absolutely blank, save that in the center of the first page there appeared the odious proclamation. Since then the governor has been recalled and, on the surface, the city is more quiet. But the startling, unhoped-for feature of this latest contest is that — for the first time in the sanguinary history of Beirut — Moslems and Christians and Jews have for the moment put aside their ancient feuds, that they might present a united front to the aggressions of the tyrannical local government. This spirit of union, even more than the desire for political reform which gave it birth, promises a new era of peace and prosperity for the most progressive city of beautiful, blood-stained Syria.

As has been said, however, the ordinary traveler sees no evidences of strife in the streets of Beirut. The largest and most conspicuous class of people whom he meets are not assassins or revolutionists, but students. This is no new thing, for the city has long been famous as a seat of learning. From the third to the sixth centuries A. D., its law school was the greatest in the Roman Empire, excelling even that of the capital and numbering its students by the thousand. One of the three commissioners who prepared the *Institutes* of Justinian was Professor Dorotheus of Beirut. In the early Saracen centuries, also, the city attained much scholarly fame and sent forth many of the foremost authorities on Moslem law and doctrine.

At the present day it is the greatest educational center in the Near East. Besides the schools maintained by each of the native churches and the mosque-schools and government academies, and institutions supported — presumably for political reasons — by Italy and Russia, there are schools or colleges of the French Sisters of Charity, Sisters of the Holy Family, Ladies of Nazareth, Lazarists, Franciscans, Capuchins and Jesuits, the German Deaconesses of Kaiserswerth, the British Syrian Mission, the Church of Scotland Mission to the Jews, and the American Presbyterian Mission, not to mention a number of others which have been organized by private individuals of missionary and philanthropic spirit. The total number of students who are being educated along modern lines is over twenty thousand.

Yet in this city of schools and colleges, if the stranger tells his coachman to drive to *el-Kulliyet* — "the College"— he will be taken without question to an institution which is incorporated under the laws of the State of New York; and a short visit here will show why this is acknowledged to be *the* college of Beirut. Upon a beautifully situated campus of fifty acres, twenty imposing stone buildings house the seven departments of what is really a large, well-equipped university of eighty instructors and nearly a thousand students, with observatory and library and scientific laboratories and hospitals, as well as literary, dramatic, musical and scientific societies and its own printing-press and monthly magazine.

Many important things are being learned and done at the Syrian Protestant College; but what strikes the observant visitor as most admirable of all is the spirit of the institution, a spirit of thoroughness and manliness and loyal fraternity and encouraging optimism. More than anything else in Beirut — yes, more than anything else in western Asia — the "S. P. C.," as its students and alumni call it, stands for the best gifts of Western civilization and for a new hope which, lighted first in beautiful Syria, is already beginning to shine on many a land far out of sight of heavenward-reaching Lebanon.

CHAPTER IV

THE SPIRIT OF OLYMPIA

MOUNT LEBANON looks to-day upon such a contest as it has never seen before. Yet Syria has witnessed many struggles. From the time men first began to fight, this land has hardly had opportunity to learn what peace and quiet mean. There are people on the campus of the American College this afternoon who can remember when the slopes of the mountain ran with blood; some of the best sprinters know what it is to flee for their lives, and even this week there has been killing on the streets of Beirut.

The contest to-day, however, is a new thing under the Syrian sun. It is not the first time that athletic games have been held — there was a field-day as far back as 1898 — but this time the preparations have been of an unusual character. During the whole week, men have been busy rolling and marking the track and removing every stick and pebble from the football field. The classrooms have been emptied of all their chairs and benches, and the faculty committee has erected four grand stands, seating over a thousand people. These will not begin to accommodate all the spectators, however, and students living in dormitories that front on the athletic field find that they have suddenly become very popular among the ladies of the city.

The football teams have ordered sweaters and shin-guards from England, and the Beirut tailors have been puzzling their brains over queerly shaped garments for the sprinters. The medals on exhibition in the college library were struck in Boston especially for this occasion, and bear on their faces the college emblem, a cedar of Lebanon. Besides the prizes for each event, the American consul will give a gold medal to the champion all-round athlete. Best of all, the governor of Lebanon has promised to attend and has sent his famous military band to provide the afternoon's music. When to these various good things is added the glory of a Syrian spring-time, and a campus set high on a bluff overlooking the blue Mediterranean, with Mount Lebanon raising its snow-capped summits high in the background, it is an occasion and a setting to quicken the slowest pulse.

To-day is so full of excitement, however, that nobody thinks very much of anything outside the athletic field. The governor's band has come early, with all kinds of instruments, especially those which make a very loud noise. A tent has been erected for them in the center of the field, and over the tent is a little American flag. The East is always so incomprehensible and contradictory that it occasions no particular surprise that a Syrian military band should be playing Sousa marches under the American colors.

But it looks as if we had at last succeeded in making the East hustle a little. All Beirut seems to be crowding into the campus. It is almost a part of his religion for an Oriental never to do anything on time; yet the grand stands are already full, and the soldiers stationed at the gate-house can hardly hold the crowds back long enough for the porter to collect their tickets. The scene is dazzling, dizzying, bewildering, like Coney Island and the Derby and the Yale-Princeton game all jumbled together.

There must be at least five thousand strangers on the college grounds, and every color of the spectrum is here, especially the very brilliant ones. The military band, with their blue uniforms and red fezes, seem almost shabby and dull in comparison with the more garish coloring all around them. The seats are mostly filled with women, whose showy dresses are hideous individually and beautiful as part of the general color scheme. Moslem harems are here with their weird veils, and there are many pretty Levantines in rich, inappropriate silks and satins. In Syria, however, the ladies do not monopolize the bright garments. Handsome young Turkish officers swagger along under yards of gold lace, merchants from the city are wearing their best and baggiest satin trousers and embroidered waistcoats and broad silk sashes, while the sons of Egyptian millionaires sport the elegantly fitting coats and tinted vests which now form the favorite costume of the streets of Cairo. The color spreads over the field and up the grand stands, with bright splashes along the sides of the dormitories. Long strips of red and white bunting flaunt the college colors; American and British and Greek and Turkish flags wave above, and the students' windows are decorated with their national emblems or class banners.

Early in the afternoon an American tutor, while ushering the women of a Moslem harem across the campus, suggested, in rather labored Arabic, that they pass around the back of one of the dormitories so as to avoid the crowd. Imagine his surprise and consternation when one of the ladies replied, "No, thank you; I'd rather go around in front"— and said it in perfect English, with just a suspicion of a Yankee twang! Who was hidden behind that black veil? What foolish, tragic venture had brought it about that an American girl should dwell behind the latticed windows of a Moslem seraglio?

But the students have no intention of being obscured by their guests. They are out a thousand strong, with their best clothes and their loudest voices. They represent every race and tongue and faith of the Near East, with here and there a stranger from Europe or South America. At first thought, it seems as though they could never be amalgamated, even for an afternoon. Here, for example, are a dozen names, representing as many nationalities; Hafiz Abd-ul-Malik, Neshan Hamyartsumian, Ahmed Zeki, Basileios Theodoropolous, Tahir Huseini, Carlos d'Oliveira, Aldo Villa, Mordecai Elstein, Emmanuel Mattsson, Joseph Miklasievicz, Eugène Faure, Emile Kirchner. As to religion, they are Moslems, Jews, Druses, Babites, and Christians of every sect. Some of the languages they speak are Arabic, Turkish, Armenian, Chaldean, Persian, Greek, Yiddish, English, Swedish, Bulgarian, Abyssinian, Italian, German, French, Portuguese, Spanish, Polish and Russian. As to geographical distribution, they come from the Balkans in the north and from Baghdad, forty days' journey to the east; from a thousand miles up the Nile, and from New York and Brazil in the west.

Probably no other institution in the world includes such a mixture of antagonistic peoples and religions, and, until quite recently, the members of each of the more largely represented races kept closely together. It used to be seldom that a Jew, for instance, associated with an Armenian outside of class hours. In the evenings the Greek students would gather in one another's rooms, or march around the campus arm in arm, singing their national songs. The Egyptians, most of whom were of very wealthy families, promenaded together, discussing the fleshpots of

Students of the American College celebrating an athletic victory

The Cape of Beirut viewed from Mount Lebanon

Cairo. Even among the Syrians, who have always formed the majority of the student body, there were lines of division between the men from Tripoli in the north and from Sidon or Jedeideh in the south. If these groups are considered as being separated by latitudinal lines, there were also the longitudinal divisions between Christian and Moslem and Jew; and sometimes long-cherished feuds broke into flame and pitched battles took place on the campus.

Not the least benefit arising from the introduction of American athletic sports has been a weakening of these ancient racial and religious barriers. The antagonisms still exist, strong and danger-breeding; but there has been a large advance made toward a more catholic college spirit. It would not be true to say that athletics has been the only cause, or even the chief cause of this change; for by precept and example, by religious instruction and social intercourse, the faculty are continually molding the characters of these young men. Yet it is true that in the case of more than one recalcitrant student whom no other influence seemed able to touch, the latent manliness has been brought out through his newly awakened interest in sports.

Most Orientals are very averse to physical exercise. Their traditional idea of enjoyment is to sit under an awning, drinking coffee and playing backgammon. That a man should go out and run around a track in shameless nakedness, and this with no hope of gain, only strengthens their conclusion that all Franks are mad. The Syrians are an imitative people, however, and some years ago the influence of the younger instructors tempted a few of the preparatory boys out for foot-races. But you cannot run a hundred-yard dash with long, baggy trousers and a silk robe which flops about your ankles. Even if you "gird up the loins" by tucking your skirts into your sash, the effect is more startling than speedy. Soon, one by one, the students ordered trousers from the city tailors. At first these garments were poorly cut and viewed with suspicion; but to-day there are hardly three men in the academic and graduate departments who wear the native costume outside of their rooms, and many of the students dress with an elegance that their professors cannot afford to emulate.

It was football, however, that did the most toward unification of the heterogeneous student body. The value of team-work is a comparatively new idea to western Asia and eastern Europe. Since the days of Alcibiades and Absalom the old ideal has been that of "every man for himself." If it had not been so, the history of the world might have been different. It was comparatively easy to understand the joy of winning a foot-race or a tennis tournament; but to play an untheatrical part in a match, obeying the captain and working for the good of the team — that was a very different thing. The students always play the association game, and it used to be the ambition of every youth to get the ball, and carry it down the field all by himself, while the audience cheered, "Bravo, bravo!" So the faculty arranged matches with the crews of visiting British warships, and from sad experience the college learned the value of side plays and frequent passes, and began to see dimly that good football is played, not with the legs and mouth alone, but with the head, and that hard team-work is better than grand stand exploits.[1] That lesson may some day change the map of Asia.

The physical director of the college now has under his charge no fewer than eighteen football teams, besides twelve basketball teams, six hockey teams, four baseball teams and a cross-country running club; thirty men play at cricket regularly, forty-seven hold certificates or medals of the (British) Royal Life Saving Society, and there are a hundred and thirty-five entries for to-day's field and track events.[2]

It makes one homesick to hear the cheers. With the exception of an occasional "meet" with some mission school, like those at Jerusalem and Sidon, there is no opportunity to compete with rival institu-

[1] In 1913, the college team defeated the champions of the British Mediterranean Fleet.

[2] The above figures are for the current year, 1913. With this exception, however, the chapter is not in any sense a composite, but describes the happenings of one actual field-day held during the author's residence in Beirut.

tions. Indeed, there is no other college in the Near East which would have any chance of winning in competition with the " S. P. C." So the enthusiasm finds a vent in cheering for the various schools of the university and for the class champions. Three of the departments — the preparatory, academic and medical — are each as large as many an American college. The competition among these runs very high, and to-day a banner is to be given to the one whose members shall score most points. Now the various department " yells " have stopped for a moment, and an upper classman starts the college cheer, just as inane to read and just as soul-stirring to hear as are those of Harvard or Yale or Princeton. There is a good deal of singing, too. The college song, like that of Cornell, is set to the tune of " Annie Lisle," but the words are full of local allusions —

" Far, far above the waters
Of the deep blue sea,
Lies the campus of the college
Where we love to be.

" Far away, behold Keneiseh!
Far beyond, Sunnin!
Rising hoary to the heavens,
Clad in glorious sheen."

Suddenly an usher comes running from the gatehouse with the news that the governor's carriage is in sight. It can hardly be true, however; for it still lacks a few minutes of two o'clock, and it would be contrary to Syrian custom for an official of such exalted rank to arrive at the same time with ordinary people. Probably he will come at about three o'clock, and stay a half hour or so, just to assure the college of his good-will. Indeed, this will be the first time that a governor has even put in an appearance at the annual games. But, after all, the usher is right. The pasha is coming — three minutes ahead of time! There is hardly a consul on the dignitaries' platform; even the American representative has not arrived yet, and there would be no one properly to welcome the governor, if the president of the college did not throw dignity to the winds and sprint across the campus to meet him.

The escort rides in at a slow canter, with sabers glistening and accouterments clattering. First come young officers, handsome and foppish, their bosoms heavy with gold lace and medals, and their Arab stallions snorting and prancing; then follows the guard of grizzled, sunburned Lebanon soldiers, clothed in blue Zouave uniforms and holding repeating-rifles across the pommels of their saddles. Behind the soldiers are carriages containing the members of the staff and their ladies; and last of all, attended by out-riders, the carriage of his excellency. The pasha is a thin little old man with a gray beard and shrewd, tired eyes; and, in striking contrast to his gayly caparisoned escort, he is quietly dressed in a dark business suit. He is a Pole by birth, a Roman Catholic by religion, a Turkish soldier by profession, and a gentleman by instinct and breeding. A son of the governor is also here. He is an attaché of the Turkish embassy at Paris, and one would take him for a cultured Frenchman. The wife of the attaché is a young American woman, a member of one of our best-known and wealthiest New York families.

Among the other guests in the seats of honor are a Greek priest, a Moslem *mollah* and a Druse emir. The senior missionary is telling the professor of philosophy how Yale used to play football back in the fifties, while the lady of the German consul is talking babies to the senior missionary's wife. The Welsh doctor, who used to live in Brazil, is talking French to the Italian professor from Cairo. The exporter of Damascus rugs is swapping Dakota stories with the Syrian editor who took the Arab troupe to the Chicago Exposition.

And in the middle of the field the official announcer is lifting up a megaphone to shout across the babel of tongues:—

"Winner of the dromedary race, Saladin; second, Haroun al Raschid; third, Sinbad. The next event will be the high jump on enchanted carpets!"

At least, that is what one would expect to hear amid this brilliant theatrical setting. But instead the call comes in faultless English —

"All out for the hundred-yard dash!"

In the finals of this race there are four men; a Greek, an Egyptian and two Syrians. Khalil Meshaqah, of the medical school, wins in ten and two-fifth seconds, without spikes, and on a dirt track [3] without guiding ropes. The college is not ashamed of its athletic records. Among its prize winners this afternoon are the best jumper of the Island of Cyprus, the champion swimmer of Alexandria, and the Greek who won the hundred-meter race in the recent Pan-Hellenic Games at Athens. On the first few field-days the Greeks carried everything before them; indeed, on one occasion three Greeks from Cyprus made more points than all the other students combined. Now, however, after only a few years of training, some splendid athletes are being developed among the Syrians, Armenians and Egyptians. Of the six men who win most points to-day, four are Syrians, one is a Greek and one is a Scotchman.

The announcer comes out again into the center of the field and shouts through his megaphone, first in English and then in Arabic —

"The discus has just been thrown one hundred and ten feet, breaking the college record!"

So the campus bursts into a new uproar of shouting and singing, and the students make quite unnecessary inquiries as to "What's the matter with McLaughlan?" while somebody tries to explain

[3] Since this record was made, a new athletic field with a cinder track has been laid out adjoining the campus.

what it is all about to the Turkish governor, who understands neither English nor Arabic, and the governor's daughter-in-law looks as if she were thinking of Travers Island.

It would take too long to describe all the events of the day: how Nedrah Meshaqah wins the thousand-yard "campus race," how Iatrou keeps the shot-put in the Greek ranks, or how Bedr breaks the record for the high jump. The real significance of the occasion is that it is all so like the field-meets of our American colleges at home.

The only typically Syrian event is the jareed-throw — and the javelin has since been included among American field-events. The jareed is a blunt dart about four feet long and an inch in diameter, and it is always thrown underhand. The Arabs use it in various games, somewhat as the old Greeks employed the javelin. At the college it is thrown for distance; and this is one of the most interesting contests, as it requires not only strength and quickness but a peculiar knack which it is almost impossible for a foreigner to learn. It looks very easy to one who has tossed baseballs all his life; yet when the American first attempts to throw the short, light stick, he sends it whirling around like a windmill. But watch that young Druse sheikh, as he carefully balances the jareed upon his finger, and then grasps it gently but firmly at the approved spot. A few slow swings of the arm to get the direction, a lean backward until the stick nearly touches the ground behind, then a jump forward and a throw so long that his hand moves fully nine feet in a straight line before it lets the missile go with a furious rifling motion — and the jareed darts up and off with a queer little nervous twist like an angry snake, and drops nearly two hundred feet away, with a force that would have broken a man's skull.

It is a proud moment for thirty Eastern athletes when they step up to the platform where the governor and his staff are sitting, and receive their medals from the Norwegian wife of the American consul and the American daughter-in-law of the Turkish pasha. Everything is over now except the football game, and the governor has stayed through it all, thus giving a most signal mark of his interest and approval. He indicates his wish to retire, and the crowd gives way for his escort. The carriages drive up to the grand stand with much snapping of whips, and the outriders prance gayly around on their restive Arabs. But just then the football teams run out into the field, resplendent in their new uniforms; and the governor repents of his decision to leave, sinks back into his seat and motions the carriages to drive away.

The captain of the medical team is a great, bearded Syrian, six feet tall. The captain of the collegiate eleven is two inches taller, also a Syrian in name and very proud of his country and race, but with a sense of humor and a knowledge of team-work which he probably inherited from his American mother. One of the full-backs is a very sturdy fellow who was born in Cyprus of a French mother and speaks Greek as his native tongue; but there is a canny twinkle in his eye and a burr in his speech which make it seem quite natural that his name should begin with "Mac." Many brilliant plays are made by the son of an Egyptian millionaire, the Druse sheikh who won the jareed throw, and an American from Jerusalem. The collegiate eleven is composed of four Syrians, three Egyptians, an Armenian, a Scotchman, an American and an Austrian; but racial and religious differences are forgotten as they play together for the honor of their side. It is a hard game, yet a very fair one, and when the "Medics" win by a score of two goals to one, even the college men lustily cheer the victors.

As the gay-colored crowd breaks over the field, his fellow-students seize the captain of the winning team and carry him around on their shoulders, singing and shouting all the while. Medical banners wave, medical hats and fezes are thrown into the air and medical men cheer until they can cheer no more. Soon the other students join in, and department rivalries are forgotten in a loud enthusiasm for *alma mater*. At the dinner hour the usual rules of decorum are for once relaxed, and the happy pandemonium continues until bedtime. Then at last, tired and sleepy and voiceless, the college settles down to a long rest, after the best field-day that has ever been held in the Turkish Empire.

CHAPTER V

ACROSS THE MOUNTAINS

RAILWAYS and carriage-roads in Syria are chiefly due to French enterprise. The *Société Ottomane des Chemins de Fer de Damas, Hama et Prolongements* has less rolling stock than its lengthy name might lead one to expect, and its slow schedule is not always observed with a mechanical Western exactness. Although Damascus is barely fifty miles from Beirut, the journey thither takes ten hours; for the constantly curving railway measures more than ninety miles and the total rise of its numerous steep grades is over 7,000 feet. This single, narrow-gauge road, which is carried over two high mountain ranges, is an admirable example of modern engineering, and the scenery through which it passes is a source of unbroken delight.

As we zig-zag up the western slope of Lebanon there appear, now at our right and now at our left, a succession of beautiful panoramas which differ one from the other only in revealing a constantly widening horizon. Rich, populous valleys, lying deep between the shoulders of the mountains, slope quickly downward to the coast where, farther and farther below us, the silvery-green olive orchards and golden sands of Beirut reach out into the ever-broadening azure expanse of the Mediterranean.

Sometimes great masses of billowing clouds drift up the valleys, so that for a while we seem to be traveling along a narrow isthmus between foaming seas. The people of Aleih — a charming summer resort where the mountainside is so steep that there is no room for a curve and the train has to back up the next leg of the ascent — are the butt of many a popular tale. One day, so the wits of the neighboring villages relate, these foolish fellows mistook the rising tide of mist for the sea itself, and the whole populace prepared to go fishing.

Another time a number of residents of Aleih went to Beirut to buy shoes. On their way back they all sat on a wall to rest; and when they were ready to go on again, behold, the new shoes were all exactly the same size, shape and color, and no man could tell which of the feet were his. So there they sat, in sad perplexity as to how they should ever reach home, until a passer-by, to whom they explained their difficulty, smote the shoes smartly one after the other with his stick and thus enabled each person to recognize his own feet.

A third Aleih story also exemplifies the ridiculous exaggeration which so delights a Syrian audience. It seems that the only public well in the village used to be the subject of frequent quarrels between the inhabitants of the upper and lower quarters. So finally the sheikh stretched a slender pole across the middle of the opening and commanded that thenceforth each of the two opposing factions was to draw only from its own side. For a time all went peace-

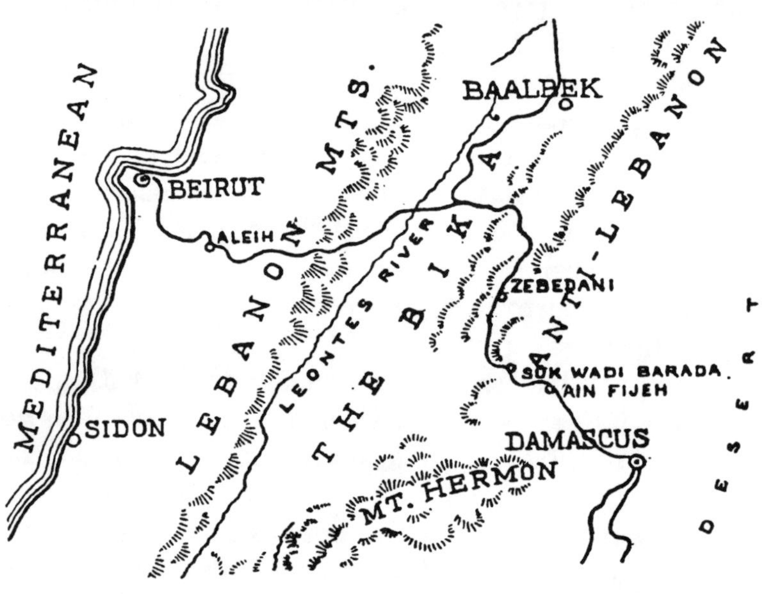

ably; but one dark night a zealous partisan was discovered diligently at work dipping water from the farther side of the pole and pouring it into his half of the well!

Shortly after leaving Aleih, the train turns straight east and climbs with labored puffings up the shoulder of Jebel Keneiseh to the watershed, 4,800 feet above

Beirut. It is very much cooler now. In midsummer, refreshing breezes blow down from unseen snowbanks among the mountaintops. In winter — if, indeed, the traffic is not entirely blocked by drifts which choke the railway cuts — the journey is memorable for its piercing, inescapable cold, and the natives who gather idly at the stations wear heavy sheepskin cloaks and keep their heads and shoulders swathed in thick shawls, though, strangely enough, their legs may be bare and their frost-bitten feet protected only by low slippers.

At last the jolting of the rack-and-pinion ceases, the train quickens its speed, passes through two short tunnels, swings around a high embankment; and over the crests of the lower hills we see a long, narrow stretch of level country, bordered on its farther side by a wall-like line of very steep mountains. The profile of the "Eastern Mountains"— as we behold them from this point we can hardly avoid using the Syrian name for Anti-Lebanon — seems almost exactly horizontal, and the resemblance of the range to a tremendous rampart is heightened by the massive buttresses which reach out at regular intervals between the courses of the winter torrents.

The valley before us is that which the Greeks named *Coele-Syria* or "Hollow Syria." In modern Arabic it is called the *Bika*' or "Cleft." Just as in Palestine the Jordan River and its two lakes are hemmed in by mountains which rise many thousand feet above, so in Syria the Bika‘ stretches between the parallel ranges of Lebanon and Anti-Lebanon. There is, however, one striking difference between the two valleys. That of the Jordan is a deep depression, and the mouth of the river is nearly 1,300 feet below the surface of the Mediterranean. On the other hand, the central valley of Syria throughout its entire length lies considerably above sea-level, and at its highest point reaches an elevation of about 4,000 feet. The Bika‘, which is seventy miles long

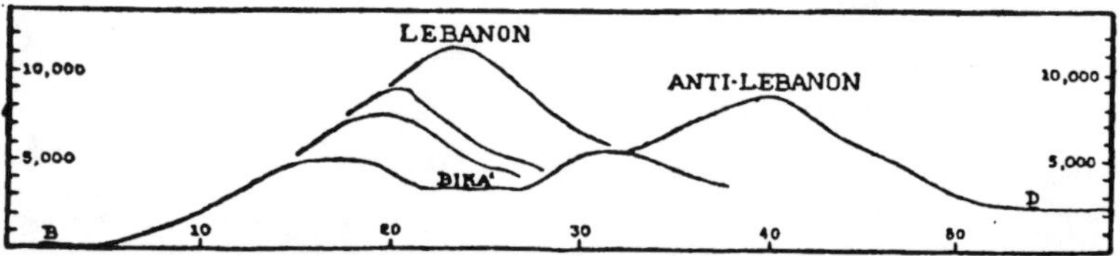

Conventionalized cross-section of Syria from Beirut (B) to Damacus (D). The horizontal distances are marked in miles, the vertical in feet.

and from seven to ten miles wide, is exceedingly fertile, and in it rise the two largest rivers of Syria. Near their sources the Orontes and Leontes pass within less than two miles of each other; yet the former flows to the north past Hama and Aleppo, while the latter turns southward and reaches the Mediterranean between Tyre and Sidon.

The Bika‘ extends north and south as far as we can see and is apparently as level as a floor.

There are hardly any trees on it, only two or three tiny hamlets and no isolated buildings. The Syrian farmers prefer to dwell on the hillsides; for there the water of the springs is cooler, it is easier to guard the villages against marauding bands, and all of the arable land below is left free for cultivation. So the great flat fields of plowed earth or ripening grain which fill the valley seem the pattern of a long Oriental carpet in rich reds and browns and greens and yellows, unrolled between the mountains.

As we pass from the shadow of a last obstructing embankment, there bursts upon our vision the glorious patriarch of Syrian peaks. Twenty-five miles to the south the splendid crest of Hermon towers into the cloudless sky a full mile above the surrounding heights.

The familiar Hebrew name of this famous mountain means the "Sacred One," and the expression "the Baal of Hermon,"[1] seems to indicate that in very ancient times it bore a popular shrine. The Jews also knew it by its Amorite title *Senir*, the "Banner." Modern Syrians sometimes refer to it as the "Snow Mountain," for its summit is capped with white long after the summer sun has melted the drifts from the lower peaks. Most commonly, however, it is called *esh-Sheikh*, which means "the Old Man," or rather "the Chieftain," for age and authority are indissolu-

[1] This is the correct rendering of Judges 3:3.

bly associated in the thought of the Arabic-speaking world.[2]

Hermon is by far the most conspicuous landmark in all Palestine and Syria. I have seen it from the north, south, east and west. I have admired it from its own near foothills and from a hundred and fifty miles away. Viewed from every side it has the same shape — a long, gently rising cone of wonderful beauty; wherever you stand, it seems to be squarely facing you; and from every viewpoint it dominates the landscape as do few other mountains in the world.

This sacred peak influenced the religious idealism of many centuries. Upon its slopes lay Dan, the farthest point of the Land of Promise. "From Dan to Beer-sheba," from the great mountain of the north to the wells of the South Country, stretched the Holy Land. Hebrew poets and prophets sang of the plenteous dew of Hermon, its deep forests, its wild, free animal life. Upon its rugged shoulders the Greeks and Romans continued the worship of the old Syrian nature-gods. Hither, in the tenth century, fled from

[2] C. R. Conder, the eminent Palestinian archæologist, points out that Arabic grammar necessitates our translating *Jebel esh-Sheikh* "Mountain *of* the Sheikh," and derives the appellation from the fact that in the tenth century the founder of the Druse religion took up his residence in Hermon (Hastings, *Dictionary of the Bible, s. v.* "Hermon"). But no one who has seen the white head of the tall, strong mountain can help thinking of Hermon as itself the proud, reverend sheikh of the glorious tribe of Syrian peaks.

Egypt Sheikh ed-Durazy and made it the center of the new Druse religion. Above its steep precipices the Crusaders built two of their largest castles. But one most solemn event of all uplifts the sacred mountain even closer to the skies; for on some unnamed summit of the "Chieftain" the supreme Leader stood when the heavens opened for His transfiguration.

We cross the valley rapidly to the junction-station of Rayak and then, again ascending, penetrate the Eastern Mountains by a winding river-course which, as we follow it higher and higher, affords fine views over the Bika' to the range of Lebanon through which we were so long traveling. Directly opposite us stands Jebel Keneiseh, bare, brown and forbidding, while beside it rises the loftier Sunnin. When viewed from the coast, this noble mountain reveals one long, even slope to its topmost crest; but its back is made up of a multitude of rounded eminences, so that it resembles an enormous blackberry. Twenty miles to the north of Sunnin, near the famous Cedars of Lebanon, the range culminates in a group of snow-capped peaks which lack the impressiveness of Hermon's haughty isolation, yet which actually rise two thousand feet above even the Sheikh Mountain.

After crossing the watershed of Anti-Lebanon, we turn south through the lovely little vale of Zebedani. At our left are the highest summits of the range; at our right are precipitous cliffs which, save for a glimpse of the snows of Hermon, shut off the distant view; but between these heights is a scene of quiet, comfortable beauty. The tract is well-watered and fertile, and its wheat-fields are as level as the surface of a lake. Indeed, there surely must have been a lake here once upon a time. Along the eastern edge of the grain-land are charming, green-hedged gardens and closely planted orchards and long lines of poplar trees, while low-bent vines hug the sunny slopes at the mountain's foot. This high but sheltered valley is one of the few places in Syria where really fine apples are grown, and the grapes and apricots of Zebedani are famous throughout the whole country.

In a small marshy lake among the hills that border the rich, slumbrous little plain there rises one of the world's greatest rivers; great not in size — at its widest it is hardly more than a mountain brook and no ship has ever sailed its waters — but great because it has made one of the proudest cities of earth; for this slender stream which winds so leisurely through the wheat-fields of Zebedani is the far-famed Abana, and Abana is the father of Damascus.

At the lower end of the valley, the brook turns sharply eastward through a break in the mountains, and we follow it swiftly down a succession of narrow chasms and wild ravines, all the way to the end of our journey. The first two hours of our ride we traveled but twelve miles: the last two hours we slide forty miles around short, confusing curves. Sometimes there are distant views of bare, reddish summits; often we are hemmed in by the dense growth of trees which border the stream; but we are never far from the rushing waters of the Abana.

There is ancient history along our route, not to speak of legends innumerable. The little village of Suk Wadi Barada or "Barada Valley Market," was once called Abila, and was the chief city of the Tetrarchy of Abilene, the fixed date of whose establishment helps us to compute the chronology of the Gospels.[3] The valley itself is still known here as Abila; and therefore, through a characteristic confusion of names, the Moslems locate the grave of Abel on the summit of an adjoining hill. Cain, they say, was at his wits' end how to dispose of the dead body of his brother, for burial was of course unknown to him; so the murderer carried the corpse on his back many days, seeking in vain a place where he might securely conceal the evidence of his crime. At last, according to the Koran, "God sent a raven which scratched upon the ground, to show him how he might hide his brother's corpse."[4]

Across the ravine from Suk Wadi Barada we can see the remains of an ancient road hewn in the solid rock, and a ruined aqueduct which some say was built by Queen Zenobia to carry the water of the Abana across the desert to Palmyra. It is almost certain, however, that both road and aqueduct, as well as the tombs whose openings appear higher up

[3] Cf. Luke 3:1. [4] Sura 5:34.

in the cliff, were constructed in the second century by the Romans.

Ain Fijeh, the next important village, bears a peculiarly redundant name, which reminds us of German Baden-Baden. The first first word is Arabic and the second is a corruption of the Greek *pege*, and both mean "spring." But, after all, "Spring Spring" is not such a bad name; for there gushes from a cave in the rock such an abundant fountain that the Abana here increases threefold in volume, and mediæval Arab geographers, as well as the modern inhabitants of the mountains, are unanimous in considering this the principal source of the river. From the cold, clear spring, a small tile aqueduct has for the last few years carried drinking-water to Damascus. Unfortunately, however, only a few of the more important buildings are as yet supplied from this source, and the common people are loath to journey to the public fountains when there are all over the city so many nearer — and dirtier — streams from which to draw. "The Moslems, especially, prefer to drink water which runs in the open rather than that which is piped," said a native physician in answer to my questions as to the health of Damascus. "So, you see," he added facetiously, "my practice has not suffered appreciably since the completion of the aqueduct."

As we descend the narrow, winding valley of the Abana, it becomes more and more choked with

An old bridge over the Barada River

Cascade falling over the edge of the Hauran into the Yarmuk Valley

verdure. We now begin to understand why the Greeks called this the *Chrysorrhoas* or "Golden River." If we take advantage of one of the lengthy stops to step across the track and plunge our hands into its icy waters, we realize the fitness of its modern Arabic name, *Baradâ* — the "Cold Stream." Occasionally we still glimpse far above us grim, treeless heights; but, between the cliffs, dense thickets or closely planted orchard trees line the river-banks. Now the Abana is a roaring, foaming torrent; now it flows chill, deep and silent; but always it hurries as if it were racing with the train. This, in its turn, goes more rapidly. It twists and swings and bumps as it takes dangerously short curves at — for a Syrian train — full speed. We pass into the shadow of a beetling precipice and, beneath the thick foliage which overhangs it, the river runs black as ink. Then, suddenly, we have left the gloom of the mountains and are out in the bright sunlight which floods a boundless plain. We have crossed to the eastern edge of Syria and before us, just beyond the orchards of Damascus, lies the desert.

CHAPTER VI

THE LAND OF UZ

TO appreciate truly the significance of Damascus, one should approach it from the east, across the thirsty wilderness which stretches between the Euphrates and the Syrian mountains. The long, wearisome journey would be worth while if only for the first glimpse of the city as it appears to the wondering eyes of the desert-dweller. But the twentieth century visitor may be excused if he prefers to save time and strength by utilizing the railway. To-day there is even a choice of routes. He can travel to Damascus from the west comfortably, or from the south speedily. But the adverbs are not interchangeable.

We have already taken the slow, beautiful journey from Beirut across the two mountain ranges. The other railway between Damascus and the coast starts from the seaport of Haifa, at the foot of Mount Carmel, and follows at first a fairly easy grade through the historic Plain of Esdraelon to the Jordan Valley at Beisan. From here it runs northward along the river to the Sea of Galilee,[1] then in a general easterly

[1] See the author's *The Real Palestine of To-day*, chapter

direction up the valley of the Yarmuk to the plateau of the Hauran, where the Haifa branch joins the main line of the Mecca railway. Although the distance to Damascus by this route is a hundred and seventy-seven miles, or almost twice that from Beirut, the journey takes no longer. But in warm weather it is not a very comfortable trip, for more than half the time the train is below the level of the sea.

From Semakh, which lies at the southern end of the Sea of Galilee six hundred feet below the Mediterranean, the railway ascends the Yarmuk gorge through the most wild and desolate scenery imaginable. The entire region northeast of Galilee is volcanic. Prehistoric flows of molten rock extended over large areas, and the subsequent erosion of the river has cut through a solid layer of hard basalt from ten to fifty feet thick, whose perpendicular black cliffs appear in striking contrast to the irregular outlines of the softer limestone beneath.

For two hours after leaving the Sea of Galilee we do not pass a human habitation; indeed, for the first few miles there is no evidence of vegetable life except now and then a small clump of bushes at a bend of the stream. As the train puffs slowly up the bed of the steep, twisting ravine, all that can be seen is the narrow torrent rushing madly along between white walls of lime or chalk, above these a smooth, regular

XV, "The War-path of the Empires," and XVIII, "The Lake of God's Delight."

layer of shining black basalt and, as we look straight up or down the valley, a few bare, brown mountain-tops showing above the nearer cliffs. After a while, however, oleanders appear along the riverside, and for mile upon mile their thick foliage and gor-

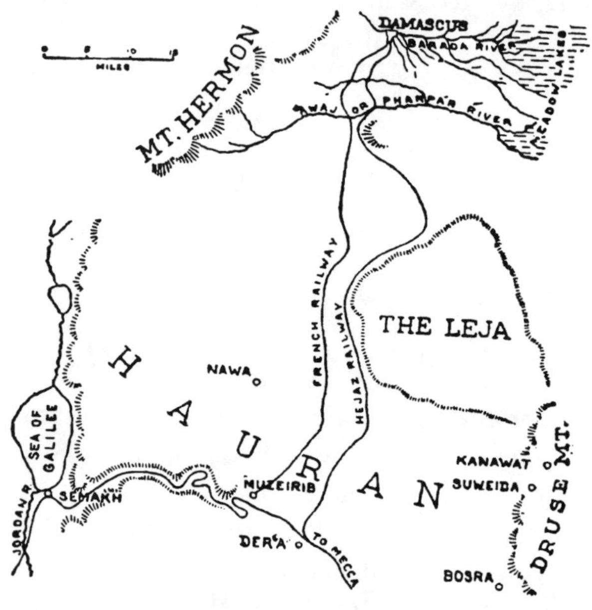

geous flowers add the one touch of life to the wild, lonely landscape. We pass a strange monolithic pyramid a hundred feet high, which has been carved by some freak of the winter floods. A little farther on, a recent landslide has covered the bottom of the valley with black stones and soot-like dust. Even early in the morning it is hot and stifling in this breezeless trench below the level of the ocean.

As we rise higher, however, scattered olive trees appear among the oleanders by the riverside, and a few little patches of thin wheat are seen among the rocks. A small herd of black, long-haired goats are drinking in the stream. We are startled to behold a rude oil-well. A dozen men are gathered at each railway station, though the villages from which they have come are still invisible on the heights above us. Then the valley suddenly turns and broadens, and we see against the cloudless sky the clean-cut profile of the highland country toward which we have been so long ascending. The track now leaves the river's bank and, in great loops, quickly mounts the side of the valley. From the edge of the plateau there comes tumbling a magnificent succession of cascades, which finally roar under a railway bridge and break in spray at the bottom of the gorge far below us. Another broader waterfall drops in a solid sheet of silver from the unseen land beyond the level summit of the precipice. Our train twists up a last steep grade, straightens out on the level ground — and, after looking for three hours at the close cliffs which hemmed in a narrow valley, it gladdens our eyes to gaze now on the vast prospect which is revealed in the shimmering light of the noonday sun.

Before us stretches the Hauran, the ancient Land of Bashan, a rolling sea of soft brownish earth and waving wheat. From time immemorial this has been the chief granary of western Asia. Until we become accustomed to the new perspective, we can not distinguish a village or tree or living creature. Here and there a few apparently low hills show their summits above the horizon. The Arabs, who came from the high eastern desert, called this the *Haurân*, or "Depression," because it lies flat between the mountains. But to us who have climbed hither from a point 2,500 feet below, the broad acres of Bashan seem set far up among the lonely skies. An endless, level, undivided expanse of wheat; dim summits far away; fertility and spaciousness and freedom and strong, ceaseless wind — this is the Hauran.

Muzeirib, the first station on the plateau, is the terminus of the earliest railway from Damascus to the Hauran, which was completed by the French in 1895. During recent years this has suffered severely from the competition of the Hejaz Railway begun in 1901 by Abdul Hamid; for the Turkish line is somewhat cheaper, has better connections, and enjoys the odor of sanctity. In fact, its chief avowed object is ultimately to connect Damascus with Mecca and thus provide transportation for the multitude of the Faithful who each year make the pilgrimage to the holy city. Only Moslems were employed on the construction of this sacred railway, large numbers of Turkish soldiers were detailed as guards and laborers; and, besides special taxes which were levied, voluntary subscriptions for the pious enterprise were sent in from all over the world of Islam. On account of the revolution of the Young Turks and the troublous times which followed the enforced abdication of Abd-ul Hamid, no work has been done on the railway for several years. Already, however, it extends 823 miles to Medina, which is four-fifths of the distance to Mecca; but non-Moslems are strictly forbidden to travel beyond Ma'an, 285 miles from Damascus, without a special permit from the government.

Der'a, where we join the Hejaz main-line, has since the earliest days of Christianity been identified with Edrei, the capital of Og, the giant king of Bashan.[2] Beneath the ancient citadel, which stands some distance to the south of the station, is a wonderful labyrinth of caves, with real streets and shops as well as dwelling-places. This underground city doubtless was intended as a refuge for the entire population of the capital in time of siege, but it has not been used for many centuries.

As our train now turns northward from Der'a, Mount Hermon comes into full view at our left, in all its splendor of towering summit and dazzling whiteness, and the lofty blue cone with its long streaks of summer snow stays with us for the rest of the day.

Thirty miles to our right, Jebel Hauran, also known as the "Druse Mountain," rises from the level sea

[2] Numbers 21:33.

of grain like a long, low island. At such a distance we find it difficult, even in this crystal air, to realize that the isolated mountain is really forty miles long and only a little short of six thousand feet high. It is one of the few localities in the region where are still found the once famous "oaks of Bashan."[3] Since the religious struggles which drenched Syria with blood in 1860, many thousand Druses have migrated from Lebanon to the Hauran, where the special retreat and stronghold of this proud, brave, relentless people is the mountain which bears their name. Hither they flee from the conscription; here they defy the hated tax-collector, flaunt their contempt of the weak Turkish government and, as is their wont everywhere, waste their own strength in bitter family feuds.

A very ancient and plausible Christian tradition, which since the rise of Islam has also been accepted implicitly by the Moslems, identifies the Hauran with the "Land of Uz" where dwelt the patriarch Job. Three towns on the western slopes of the Druse Mountain perpetuate his story. Bishop William of Tyre, writing in the twelfth century, mentions the popular belief that Job's friend Bildad the Shuhite dwelt at Suweida, and the inhabitants of this village boast that the patriarch himself was their first sheikh. At Kanawat a group of very old ruins is commonly known as the "Convent of Job," and at Bosra, the

[3] Isaiah 2:13, etc.

ancient capital of the Hauran, there is a Latin inscription in his praise. Probably this belonged to a sixth century leper asylum; for the suffering patriarch early came to be considered the special patron of those who, like himself, were afflicted with the most mysterious and loathsome of diseases.

But it is in the plain that memories of this Biblical drama cluster most closely. Nawa, twenty miles northwest of Der'a, has for two thousand years been honored as Job's birthplace. An hour's ride to the south of this village there stood fifteen hundred years ago a splendid church dedicated to the Man of Uz, and part of the ruined "Monastery of Job" is still in good enough condition to be used as Turkish barracks. Near by is shown the rock on which he leaned while arguing with his three friends — it is a small basalt monument erected by Rameses II.— also the stone trough in which he washed after his afflictions were ended, and the tomb of the patriarch and his wife.

In spite of the naïve and often impossible localization of particular incidents of the story of Job, it is quite possible that the very old tradition is correct, and the mysterious Land of Uz across which roamed the herds and flocks of "the greatest of all the Children of the East" was this same free, fertile tableland along which we are now traveling. Before the Hauran was so largely given over to agriculture, it must have been an ideal grazing country; it has always been subject to forays by robber tribes from the desert;[4] and the "great wind from the wilderness" which smote the dwelling of Job's eldest son[5] would perhaps nowhere else blow with such fury as on this high, open plateau.

There was just such a great wind from the wilderness the last time I went to Damascus. The Hauran bears a deserved reputation for coolness and healthfulness; but that day, as happens two or three times each summer, there was a sirocco. The wind was indeed blowing — blowing a furious gale of perhaps thirty-five miles an hour; but it came straight from the eastern desert and scorched as if it had been a blast from an opened furnace door. I did not have a thermometer with me; but, from sirocco experiences elsewhere, I should judge that the temperature in the train was not under a hundred and five degrees. The drinking-water that we had brought for the journey became warm and nauseating; but we put it to good use in soaking the back of our necks, where it evaporated so quickly in the dry, burning wind that it stung like ice for a few seconds, and then was gone. Strange as it may seem, the only other way to mitigate the heat was to shut the car windows and *keep the breeze out.*

There were fortunately some interesting incidents to enliven the long, hot ride over the monotonous plain. We did not see any of the renowned "strong

[4] Job 1:15, 17. [5] Job 1:19.

bulls of Bashan,"[6] or any other cattle grazing on the plain, but we watched slow caravans bearing wheat to the coast, as they have been doing for millenniums past. They could never carry all the grain that this productive district might harvest, and the railways should prove a rich boon to the Hauran. We pondered curiously as to why the stations were never by any chance just at the towns and why the track should swing far to the right and left in great curves, as if it were ascending a difficult grade, when the only engineering problem involved in its construction could have been solved by laying a ruler on the map and drawing a straight line down the center of the level plain. A fellow-traveler explained to us that the course of the railway had not been determined by the usual considerations, such as economy of construction and the desirability of passing through the most densely populated districts, but by the amount of *bakhsheesh* which wealthy landowners would pay the government in order to have the line pass through their estates.

We stopped an unconscionable length of time at every station, for no evident reason; and when we did get ready to start there were so many vociferous warnings that very naturally none of them was heeded by the passengers who had got off for refreshments. So finally the rapidly moving train would be chased by a crowd of excited peasants, most of whom

[6] Psalm 22:12, etc.

carried big bundles and wore long, hampering garments. Several were left behind at lonely stations. There would be another train — to-morrow! Of course, all the dogs ran after us. Provided they are well-fed, dogs and children are exactly the same the world over; and these were not the starved, sullen curs which lie in Oriental gutters, but were wide-awake, fun-loving fellows who ran merrily alongside the train for a half-mile from the town, and had no difficulty in understanding our English shouts of encouragement. As we were pulling out of one of the stations, a very reverend, gray-bearded old farmer stole a ride on the running-board; but he misjudged the quickly increasing speed of the train, and, when he at last decided to jump off, rolled head-over-heels down the steep embankment. The last we saw of him, he was gazing after us with a ludicrously dejected countenance whose every lineament expressed stern disapproval of the nervous haste of these degenerate modern days.

As a rule the other travelers were too hot and tired to afford us much entertainment; but one new arrival, not finding a seat elsewhere, tried to force his way into the harem-compartment which Turkish railways always provide for the seclusion of Moslem ladies. The lord and master of the particular harem occupying this compartment resented the intrusion with such a frenzy of threatening gesticulation and insulting malediction that the members of our party who

Long, slow caravans have always been crossing the Hauran

Damascus in the midst of its far-reaching orchards

were unaccustomed to the ways of the East expected to see murder committed forthwith. The conductor, who interposed as peace-maker, was — as is usual on this holy railway — a Turk who knew no Arabic, and he consequently had great difficulty in determining what the quarrel was about; but the Syrians have a healthy fear of any one wearing a uniform, so the trouble was finally adjusted without bloodshed.

After we became accustomed to the peculiar features of the landscape we could now and then distinguish a village. Yet at a very short distance the largest settlements were blurred into the brown plain; for the houses are all built of a dull black basalt and, save for one or two square towers, the compact hamlets are hardly to be distinguished from rough outcroppings of rock. All of the dwellings look like deserted ruins: some of them are. All seem centuries old: many have been occupied for more than a thousand years, for the hard basalt seems never to crumble.

The extraordinarily rich earth of the Hauran is only disintegrated lava, and as we near the end of the plain we pass tracts where presumably more recent eruptions have not yet been weathered into fertile soil. Two or three miles to the east of the railway a long line of dark rock some thirty feet high marks the western edge of the Leja, which in New Testament times was known as the Trachonitis [7] or "Rocky

[7] Luke 3:1.

Place." From now-extinct volcanoes at the northern end of the Druse Mountain there flowed these three hundred and fifty square miles of lava, which has broken in cooling into such a maze of irregular fissures that its surface has been likened to that of a petrified ocean. Yet this rugged region contains also little lakes, and pockets of arable soil, and numerous ruins of villages and roads and bridges which point to a considerable population in former days. *Lejâ* means " hiding-place " or " refuge," and the Druses call this forbidding district the " Fortress of Allah." The entire lava mass is honeycombed with caves. Indeed, the people of the Hauran say that one who knew the labyrinth of subterranean passages could make his way from one end of the Leja to the other without once appearing above ground. It is no wonder that this immense natural citadel, with its unmarked trails, its innumerable hiding-places in dark caves or deep-cut fissures of the rock, and its easy dominance over the dwellers on the level plain below, has always been a thorn in the side of whatever government pretended to rule the Hauran. Eighty years ago the Druses of the Leja, although they were outnumbered by the attacking force twenty to one, routed with terrible slaughter the entire army of Ibrahim Pasha, the great Egyptian conqueror.

The description of the Leja and its inhabitants which was written in the first century A. D. by Josephus would serve for any period in its wild history.

"It was not an easy thing to restrain them, since this way of robbery had been their usual practice, and they had no other way to get their living, because they had neither any city of their own, nor lands in their possession, but only some receptacles and dens in the earth, and there they and their cattle lived in common together: however, they had made contrivances to get pools of water, and laid up corn in granaries for themselves, and were able to make great resistance by issuing out on the sudden against any that attacked them; for the entrances of their caves were narrow, in which but one could come in at a time, and the places within incredibly large and made very wide; but the ground over their habitations was not very high, but rather on a plain, while the rocks are altogether hard and difficult to be entered upon unless any one gets into the plain road by the guidance of another, for these roads are not straight, but have several revolutions. But when these men are hindered from their wicked preying upon their neighbors, their custom is to prey one upon another, insomuch that no sort of injustice comes amiss to them."[8] Josephus' diction is as involved as the labyrinthine trails of the Leja, but his facts are still correct.

Further evidences that we are in a volcanic region are found in the round black stones, about the size of large bowling-balls, which now begin to appear on the plain. At first they do not seriously interfere

[8] *Antiquities of the Jews*, XV. 10.1.

with cultivation, for the farmers gather them into heaps along the edges of their fields. A few miles farther on, however, there are so many that there has been no attempt to remove them and the light plow has simply scratched whatever narrow strips of earth might lie between the rocks. At last they cover the land as far as we can see, with hardly their own diameter separating them. There must be ten thousand of them to the acre. Millions upon millions of black spots dot the nearer landscape and in the distance merge into an apparently solid mass of dark, hard sterility.

By this time most of the passengers in our coach have become very tired and irritable, though the loud breathing of some indicates that they have fallen into a restless slumber. Several are quite sick from the heat. At half-past five in the afternoon the sun has lost none of its midday glare, and the noisy wind from the desert still scorches with its furnace breath. On either side, the monotonous multitude of round black rocks strew the brown, burnt earth. The hills, which constantly draw in closer to us, seem as if they might have fair pasture-land on their lower slopes; but, save for the shining white dome of one Moslem tomb, they bear nothing higher than scattered grass and dusty thorn-bushes. We climb slowly over the watershed in the narrow neck of the plain, then speed swiftly down a steep incline; and, lo, we behold a veritable paradise of running water and heavily laden orchard trees, above which the glory of the setting sun gilds a forest of slender minarets.

CHAPTER VII

THE EARTHLY PARADISE

According to the Moslem wise men, Jebel Kasyun is a very sacred mount; for upon it Abraham dwelt when there was revealed to him the supreme doctrine of the unity of God. Long before that, however, Adam lived here: some say that he was formed from the earth of this very mountain, and that the reddish streaks upon its sides are nothing less than the indelible bloodstains of murdered Abel.

Yet as we stand by the little shrine known as the Dome of Victory, which crowns the summit, we are not thinking of ancient legends. Below us lies a scene of entrancing interest and of a peculiar beauty which is unlike that of any other beautiful prospect in the world.

Back of us are the mighty, rock-buttressed Mountains of the East, from whose sterile heart is rent a deep, dark ravine which thunders with the cascades of the Abana. Then, issuing from its narrow defile, Abana is suddenly tamed. It spreads fan-like into seven quiet branches; and these in turn divide and subdivide into a myriad life-giving streams which sink at last in wilderness sands, but, ere they sink, make the desert to rejoice and blossom as the rose.[1]

In the foreground of the picture, Damascus seems like an immense silver spoon laid on a piece of soft, green plush. The long, slender handle, which is made up of the modern peasant-markets, stretches away two miles southward. The nearer bowl is the site of the ancient city. Above its monotonous succession of solidly massed houses are seen high, cylindrical roofs which cover the most important bazaars; in the very center stands the famous Omayyade Mosque with its splendid dome and spacious court and three lofty towers, while a multitude of other graceful minarets — it is said that they are exactly as many as the days of the year — rise above the most mysterious and fascinating of Moslem capitals. Surely the traveler must be ignorant of history and bereft of sentiment who does not feel a deep, strange thrill as he first looks upon the great city

[1] It is the Abana, or Barada, which waters by far the greater portion of this fertile district. The identification of the Pharpar, which Naaman mentioned also as one of the "rivers of Damascus" (II Kings 5:12), is uncertain. It may have been one of the branches into which the Abana divides as it passes through the city. More probably, however, it was the river now known as the Awaj; for this is the only other stream in the vicinity whose size is comparable to that of the Abana and, though it flows some seven miles south of Damascus, it is used for irrigating a considerable tract of the surrounding orchard-country.

which since the dawn of history has sat in proud strength between the mountains and the desert.

From the viewpoint of physical geography, Syria is Lebanon; but politically, commercially and socially, it is still true that "the head of Syria is Damascus."[2] Indeed, the city is now hardly ever called by its real name, *Dimeshk.* It is simply *esh-Shâm*— Syria!

History does not recall a time when Damascus did not nestle here among the orchards which sweep out to the edge of the desert. The Moslem tradition that it was founded by Eliezer, the chief servant of Abraham, points to far too late a date. Josephus tells us that it was built by Uz, the grandson of Shem the son of Noah, and that when Abraham came hither from Ur with an army of Chaldeans, he captured the already old capital and for a time reigned here as king of Syria.[3] "The name of Abram is even now famous in the country of Damascus," adds the Jewish historian. Eighteen hundred years later, that is still true.

Without discussing further its legendary claims to supreme antiquity, it is safe to say that Damascus is the oldest important city in the world with an unbroken history reaching to the present day. The fame of its artificers and gardeners is embodied even in our English language; for we speak of Damascus steel, the damask plum, damask rose, damask color,

[2] Isaiah 7:8. [3] *Antiquities of the Jews,* I.6.4; I.7.2.

damask decoration and damaskeened metal-work. Many of the greatest men of earth have trodden its streets or fought before its walls or worshiped at its shrines. Abraham the Hebrew, Tiglath-pileser the Assyrian conqueror, Herod the Great, Paul of Tarsus, Khaled the "Sword of Allah," Baldwin of Flanders, Louis VII. of France, Nureddin the Syrian, Saladin the Kurd, Tamerlane the Tartar — such are only a few of the names which come to mind as we gaze upon the time-stained, battle-worn, but still rich and haughty city. To tell adequately the story of this most ancient of capitals would necessitate covering all the centuries of human history.

At the foot of the hill we shall find a tram-car waiting to take us to a modern hotel with electric lights and city-water, and in the evening we can hear a phonograph in any one of a hundred cafés, or visit moving-picture shows in the Serai Square, where a tall column commemorates the completion of the telegraph-line to Mecca. Yet, for all these recent innovations from the Western world, the real Damascus is quite unchanged. It is still the most brilliant, entrancing, fanatical and intolerant of Moslem cities, the one which best preserves the manners and customs of the early centuries of Islam. Indeed, this is to-day the typical Arabian Nights city; for Cairo, where those thrilling fairy tales were first related, is rapidly becoming Europeanized through British influence, Constantinople is thronged with Greeks and

Armenians and intimidated by foreign embassies, and the glory of Baghdad has long since departed. But Haroun al-Raschid and his faithful vizier might wander through the tortuous mazes of the bazaars of Damascus and recognize hardly an essential change from the life of a Moslem capital of a thousand years ago.

Its Oriental characteristics have been thus preserved, and will doubtless be preserved for many years to come, because of all great Arabic-speaking cities Damascus is least dependent on the West. An impassable wall might cut it off entirely from intercourse with Europe, and still it would thrive and wax strong on the wealth of its own orchards and its commerce with the lands across the Syrian desert.

As we view the wide prospect from the Dome of Victory, the city seems a whitish island, half hidden by the billows of an ocean of luxuriant foliage. Far as the eye can see — far as the dim blue hills which mark the eastern horizon — the plain is flooded with leaves and blossoms. At closer view we shall recognize the fig and pomegranate, the mulberry, pistachio, peach, almond and apricot, the tall poplar and waving cypress and bending grape-vine and short, gnarled olive tree. But from Jebel Kasyun we perceive only one great expanse of warm, rich verdure; all shapes and colors are merged into a soft, level green.

Behind us rise the bare, chalky cliffs of Anti-

Lebanon. Beyond those low azure hills at the east is the cruel desert. But between the mountains and the desert hills lies the hundred square miles of the *Ghûta*—the "Garden" of Damascus. No language is too extravagant for the Arabic writers who describe this land of fruits and flowing waters. It is "the most excellent of all the beautiful places of earth," exclaims the learned Abulfeda; and the famous geographer Idrisi says, "There are grown here all sorts of fruits, so that the mind cannot conceive the variety, nor can any comparison show what is the fruitfulness and excellence thereof, for Damascus is the most delightful of God's cities in the whole world." Indeed, this is the place which, among all the habitations of men, comes nearest to the description of the Moslem paradise—

"The people of the Right Hand!
Oh, how happy shall be the people of the Right Hand! . . .
In extended shade,
And by flowing waters,
And with abundant fruits,
Unfailing, unforbidden . . .
Gardens beneath whose shades the rivers flow."[4]

The prophet who sang thus of the celestial delights of the Faithful once stood, it is said, on the summit of this sacred mountain and gazed with won-

[4] The *Koran,* Sura 56:26f; 61:12.

dering admiration, as we are gazing, on the bounteous splendor of the Garden of Damascus. But Mohammed refused to go down into the city for fear lest, having tasted the joys of this earthly paradise, he might lose his desire for the heavenly.

CHAPTER VIII

THE PORT OF THE WILDERNESS

ALTHOUGH it is ninety miles by railway from navigable water, Damascus partakes of the characteristics of a seaport. It is, in fact, the port of the wilderness. Just to the east of its fertile "garden" is the Syrian desert, across which slow caravans have always been coming and going — traveling from the rich river-bottoms of Mesopotamia, from Persia and India, and even from far distant China, to bring the riches of Asia to the overflowing warehouses of Damascus. The lands from which the city derives its prosperity cannot compete with European industries, and so only a small proportion of their products is now sent westward across the Mediterranean. Yet Damascus remains still the metropolis of the desert peoples. From the viewpoint of the peasant or Bedouin Arab, it is a very modern place; and to the stranger who can see beneath the alluring glamour of its Orientalism, its chief characteristics are abounding prosperity and noisy activity. This oldest of cities is no mere interesting ruin or historical pageant. Even in the fast-month of Ramadan, its streets are as crowded as the most congested shopping district of London or New York or Paris.[1]

The most characteristic feature of the bazaar is its smell — that peculiar, inescapable blending of licorice and annis and pungent spices and heavy perfumes, combined with a vague odor of age and staleness which pervades the dust-laden air, and sometimes with an odor not at all vague which arises from the filth of unswept streets. It is not when I "hear the East a-callin'" but when I *smell* the East that the waves of homesickness sweep deepest over me. I love the scent of the bazaar. Sometimes I catch a whiff of it through the open door of a little basement store in the Syrian Quarter of New York; and in a moment my thoughts are five thousand miles away among the old familiar scenes.

The next most vivid impression of the bazaar is its weird combination of bright coloring and gloom. The narrow, winding street is guarded from the glaring sun by striped awnings and old carpets which reach across from house to house. Some few of the chief thoroughfares, like the "Street called

[1] Estimates of the population of the city vary from 150,000 to a more probable 300,000. Of this number, some 10,000 are Jews, 30,000 are "Greek" and "Latin" Christians, and a few score are Protestants. At least four-fifths of the population is Mohammedan, and Islam is dominant and uncompromising in Damascus, as it is not in cities like Constantinople and Cairo, where Moslem fanaticism is to a greater or less degree held in check by the constant menace of interference by Christian powers.

Straight," are enclosed by great cylindrical roofs of corrugated iron. You are indoors and yet out-of-doors. The light is dim; but it is daylight, and you feel that all the while the sun is shining very brightly overhead. Along the fronts of the shops and hanging on ropes which stretch across the street, are shining brasses and pieces of inlaid wood-work and cloths of the most gorgeous orient hues; but the rear of these same shops is usually wrapped in impenetrable gloom. Sometimes there is visible only a square black hole surrounded by a frame of gaudy silks. When you pass a blacksmith's forge, with shadowy figures moving among the sparks at the back of the inky darkness, it seems like a glimpse into inferno.

Most of the shops are tiny affairs only six or eight feet square, which open on the street for their entire width and have the floor raised to about the height of the customer's waist. The resemblance of a bazaar to a long double row of pigeon-holes is increased by the manner in which the box-like recesses follow continuously one after the other, with no doorways between, as the entrance to their upper stories is by ladders in the rear.

In the middle of his diminutive emporium, the typical Damascus merchant sits all day cross-legged, smoking his water-pipe, reading from a Koran placed before him on a little wooden book-rest, and eternally fondling his beard. Frequently he says his prayers. Sometimes he varies the monotony of a dull day by chatting with a fellow-merchant in a neighboring shop fully ten feet away. The Jews and Christians of the city may be annoyingly importunate; but the Moslems, who form the large majority, seem insolently careless as to whether the passing stranger pauses to examine their goods or not. Over their places of business they hang gilded invocations to "the One who giveth sustenance," and then leave matters entirely in His hands. If nothing is sold all day, it is the will of Allah: if a customer does come, it is the will of Allah — that he shall be overcharged as much as possible.

Shopping in Damascus is not an operation to be hurried through with careless levity. If you appear a promising customer, the merchant will set coffee before you and, while you and he are drinking together, will talk about anything under the sun except business. When you ask him the price of an article, he may tell you to keep it for nothing, just as did Ephron the Hittite when Abraham was bargaining for the Cave of Machpelah.[2]

If, however, you offer a fair amount for that same "gift," he will protest that to accept such a paltry sum would necessitate his children's going hungry and naked. So he names a price about double what he expects to get, and you suggest a sum equal to half what you are willing to pay. Then follow vo-

[2] Genesis 23:11.

ciferous exclamations, indignant gesticulations, and sacred oaths, while his price slowly comes down and yours slowly goes up, until at last they almost, though not quite, meet. Neither will change his "last word" by a single piaster. Negotiations are at an end. You turn scornfully to leave the shop of the extortioner, while the merchant commends his business to God and resignedly begins to wrap up the goods and return them to their shelves. He does this very deliberately, however, and just then — because you two are such good friends, whose appreciation of noble character finds its ideal each in the other's life — you decide to split the difference, the purchase is completed, and you part with mutual protestations that only a deep, fraternal regard forces you — and him — to conclude the bargain at such a ruinous figure.

"It is bad, it is bad, saith the buyer;
But when he is gone his way, then he boasteth."[3]

Perhaps the shop-keeper will still, however, detain you for a glass of sherbet. If he does, then you have probably paid too much, after all.

A friend of mine was obliged to spend no less than two weeks in purchasing a single Persian rug; but during those two weeks the price went down ninety dollars. One winter I had occasion to buy, at different times, several small picture frames. They

[3] Proverbs 20:14.

were all exactly the same size, shape and material, were obtained from the same salesman at the same shop, and in the end I paid for them the same price to a piaster. Yet the purchase of each one necessitated a half-hour of excited bargaining.

It should be understood, however, that there is really nothing dishonest about such a procedure as that described above; for neither party is misled in the least by the other's protestations, and neither believes that he is deceiving the other. It is just the leisurely, intensely personal Oriental way of doing business. After you once become used to it, bargaining in the bazaars is far more full of excitement and human interest than buying something in the West, where fixed prices are distinctly marked. If you are so crude as to ask a Moslem merchant to tell under oath what he paid for an article, he will often speak the exact truth. But be sure to swear him by a formula which he considers binding. Every detail of a Syrian business transaction is embellished by one or more of the fervent oaths of the East. The traveler from the Occident, however, needs only one: the "word of an Englishman"[4] is still accepted at face value. Indeed, a generation ago, Moslems who would unblushingly call upon almighty God to witness to the most patent falsehoods, could be trusted to speak the exact truth when they

[4] This includes the American, for all who speak the English language are ordinarily classed as *Ingleezy*.

One of the more modern avenues of Damascus

A typical Syrian Café

swore by the beard of a certain upright English merchant of Beirut.

No picture can ever adequately represent the bazaar, not even a moving picture; for besides the unending kaleidoscopic changes of coloring, as brightly dressed peddlers and purchasers move hither and thither, there is a ceaseless, deafening, indescribable and untranslatable tumult of sound. Yet to one who understands Arabic, this is more than noise: it is music, poetry and romance. The hawker of each commodity uses a peculiarly worded appeal which, in eloquent circumlocution, extols the virtues of his wares. These calls are usually rhyming; often they include one of the ninety-nine sacred titles of Allah, and frequently they are sung to a set tune. Back and forth through the perilously crowded streets they go — boys with great trays of sweetmeats on their heads, men with tubs of pickled vegetables, peasants bearing heavy loads of fresh figs, water-carriers stooping low under their goatskin bottles, peddlers of cakes and nuts and sherbets and the nosegays which the Syrian gentleman loves to hold — literally under his nose — as he strolls through the city. All are shouting their wares. "Oh, thirsty one!" "Oh, father of a family!" "Oh, Thou who givest food!" "Allay the heat!" "Rest for the throat!" When Abraham passed through Damascus he doubtless heard these same cries.

If we are driving, as is possible in the wider bazaars, our gallant coachman adds to the din as he proudly snaps his long whip, toots the strident automobile horn which is now affixed to all Damascus carriages and, in courteous gentleness or bawling rage or sighing relief, keeps up an unintermitting flow of Arabic adjuration to the passers-by whom he almost, but never quite, runs down. "Look out for your back! Hurry up, uncle! Your back, your back! — may your house be destroyed! Your right, lady! Your left, sir! Slowly, oh, inmates of the harem! Oh, pilgrim, your back! Child, beware! Your back, my friend! *Your back!* YOUR BACK! E-e-eh! A-a-ah!"

High above the other calls rises now and then the shrill, nasal song of the vender of sweetened bread, *Allah er-Razeek!* — "God is the Nourisher!" A half-naked beggar changes his pathetic whine to a lusty curse as he slinks out of the way of a galloping, shouting horseman. Any one who feels in the mood kneels down anywhere he happens to be and prays aloud. As a kind of accompaniment to the vociferous chorus there sounds the continuous tinkling of the brass bowls which are rattled against each other by the lemonade-sellers. And — very frequently in Damascus — there pierces through the deafening tumult the thin, penetrating chant of the muezzin who, from his lofty minaret or from the mosque door in the crowded, narrow street, calls to the greedy bazaar to think on the things that are unseen and eternal.

The great conflagration of 1911 destroyed the heart of the business district by the Omayyade Mosque, and those who knew the city of a few years ago find it sadly strange to climb over the heaps of dusty rubbish which cover once familiar streets. But during the rebuilding, which is progressing rapidly, there is no appreciable diminution of business, and the intricate maze of the bazaars still presents scenes of marvelous variety and endless fascination. There is the Water-pipe Bazaar, where *narghileh* bowls are made out of cocoanuts ornamented with gold and silver, the Draper's Bazaar filled with shoddy European stuffs, the Saddle Bazaar with its brightly covered Arabic saddles and gorgeous accouterments, the almost forsaken Bazaar of the Booksellers, where now hardly a half-dozen poorly stocked booths hint at the intellectual conquests of the Damascus of centuries gone by, and the Spice Market, whose long rows of bottles scent the air with their essences and attars. The Silk Bazaar is the most brilliant, and its gaudiest patterns are hung out for the inspection of admiring Bedouin visitors. The Second-hand Bazaar of the auctioneers is commonly known as the Louse Market, not because of the uncomplimentary suspicion which first suggests itself, but from a very small and agile coin known by that name, which is frequently used in increasing the bids.

As we pass along one street after another, we see open-front bakers' shops where paper-like loaves are sold, still hot from the oven, and confectioners' booths filled with all manner of sherbets and jellies and delicious preserved fruits and the infinite variety of sweet, indigestible pastry in which the Syrians delight. In one little square there are great piles of thin apricot paste which look exactly like bundles of brown paper. The merchant offers us a sample to taste, but we are not quite sure as to the quality of the dust that has been settling upon it all the morning. A long towel hung over yonder doorway indicates that it is the entrance to a *hammâm* or public bath, within whose steaming court we can see brown, half-naked forms reclining on dingy divans. The intricate lattice-work of overhanging balconies guards the harems of the merchants from the vulgar gaze of the crowds below. This little gate, curtained by a hanging rug and edged with a line of slippers, leads from the deafening tumult of the bazaar to the solemn quiet of a cool, spacious mosque.

From time immemorial the merchant-artisans of Damascus have been united in powerful associations. There is even a guild of beggars, though, to do them justice, these are neither so numerous nor so importunate as in most Syrian cities. On the other hand, the curs which infest the busiest streets are innumerable and are disgusting in appearance beyond any other dogs I have ever seen. Yet these sore, starved racks of bones, with hardly the energy to get out of the way of a passing carriage, have organizations of their own. At any rate, they recognize definite boundaries; and a dog who ventures outside the territory occupied by his own clan does so at peril of his life. One evening a friend of mine, who is a good mimic, was so unwise as to bark lustily just as he entered our hotel. In a moment every cur in the district was giving voice; and far into the night, as unhappily was all too strongly impressed upon us, they kept up their vociferous search for the unknown intruder.

But it is never quiet in Damascus. Most Orientals go to bed very early. Jerusalem is like a city of the dead by half-past eight in the evening. The Damascenes, however, seem to need no sleep, and the noises of the streets never cease. The only noticeable change in their volume is that, when the shops close, just before sunset, the tumult suddenly increases. Then, hour after hour, you can hear the heavy murmur of the multitude, broken occasionally by the voice of someone singing, or by a chorus of loud cheers. An interminable succession of songs and marches, all of them fortissimo and in a strident minor key, shatter what ought to be the midnight stillness as they rattle from phonographs whose

Arabic records are prepared by the German subsidiary of an American talking-machine company. Very far off, a dog lifts up his voice in a faint howl which starts a pandemonium of barks and growls and yelps all over the neighborhood. The freshening breeze rustles among the orchards; then it slams a window shut. The bell of a tram-car rings sharply; carriage horns give loud double toots which just fail of forming any known musical interval, and always there is the sound of water — rushing, purling, rippling, splashing — the eternal anthem of Damascus' greatness.

So when his second day in this noisy city draws to a close, the wise traveler decides that, as there is no use trying to get to sleep early, he will go out and himself share in the midnight enjoyments. I do not know how many cafés there are in Damascus: I should be quite ready to believe anyone who told me that there were ten thousand. They are said to be the finest in Syria. Indeed, the Damascenes boast that the first of all coffee-shops was established in their city, and also that sherbet was invented here.

The best cafés are situated beside the main branch of the Barada. Those near St. Thomas' Gate have very attractive shaded gardens, where the tables are set out under spreading trees and are surrounded by tiny streams of running water. An evening visit to one of these riverside resorts is a memorable experience, and it is quite safe; for, unless corrupted by European influence, no Moslem ever touches alcoholic beverages, and one need therefore fear none of the drunken roughness which is associated with the "cafés"— which of course are not cafés at all — of Christian America. The Damascene seeks his recreation amid an atmosphere of ease and leisure and refined enjoyment. If a patron wishes to dream away the whole evening over one cup of coffee or a five-cent *narghileh,* there is no one to object. Itinerant musicians beguile the hours of darkness with plaintive minor ditties sung to the accompaniment of the guitar or zither; story-tellers spin endless fairy tales to circles of breathless listeners, and — alas! — the tireless phonograph roars its brassy songs. Many of the regular habitués of the place are absorbed in interminable games of backgammon. Coffee, fruit syrups, pastry, candy, nuts, cool water-pipes and mild cigarettes — such are the favorite refreshments of the fierce, fanatical Moslem!

As the cups in which the coffee is served are tiny, handleless things, hardly larger than a walnut, they are usually set in holders of filigree work. These are, as a rule, made of brass, but in homes of wealth they may be silver or even gold. The liquor is often flavored with rose-water and is very thick and sweet, though it will be prepared *murr* if anyone has such an outlandish taste as to prefer it "bitter." The unpalatable sediment which fills a good third of the cup must on no account be stirred up. Many a stranger has found to his cost that the coffee is served exceedingly hot; and it is a necessity as well as a sign of good breeding to keep the lips from quite touching the surface and to suck up the drink with a loud hissing noise. In a private house, this formality should by no means be neglected, even if the coffee has become cooled, as the omission would be equivalent to a criticism of the host.

Around the coffee-pot centers the social life of the Moslem world. It has an important place in every kind of ceremonial and festive occasion, from the circumcision of the child to the funeral of the old man. The merchant offers it to his prospective customer. The desert sheikh starts his women grinding the beans in a large wooden mortar as soon as a stranger enters his tent. Not to give coffee to a guest would signify that he was unwelcome.[5] It is invariably served at the beginning of a call. Later

[5] Some years ago, our minister to Turkey, who had been promised an audience with Abdul Hamid, was made to wait half a day in an anteroom of the palace *without being offered coffee*. So far as I know, that fact was never published; for the American newspapers seem to have quite missed the significance of the omission, and our representative himself apparently did not realize that he had been publicly insulted. But the experienced diplomat who was then in charge of our Department of State cabled the minister, in case of further affront, to leave Constantinople immediately.

on, sherbet is brought in, and then the visitor knows that it is time for him to leave.

Coffee sometimes plays a more serious part in Eastern affairs. Its heavy sweetness disguises varied and deadly poisons. The bacilli of typhoid fever are said, in this scientific generation, to be drunk unsuspectingly by many a venturesome meddler in affairs of state. The death penalty is seldom inflicted in the Turkish Empire. Deposed ministers and irrepressible busybodies and troublesome reformers are merely imprisoned or exiled. Often they are sent to Damascus. Then, shortly, they die of indigestion or heart failure.

CHAPTER IX

THE RICHES OF DAMASCUS

THE great khans, or wholesale warehouses, of Damascus lie in the center of the city near the Omayyade Mosque. As a rule they are not detached structures, but are hidden by the surrounding shops and are entered through tunnels which pierce the sides of the bazaars. The finest of them is the Khan Asad Pasha, which was erected a hundred years ago by the governor whose name it bears, and is still owned by his family. This is one of the few really impressive pieces of Arabic architecture in Syria, rich and massive, yet effectively adapted to the purposes for which it was intended. The building is constructed of alternate courses of dark brown and yellow limestone, and its principal entrance is a high, vaulted "stalactite" gateway covered with beautiful carvings. The central court is a hundred feet across and, as one comes suddenly from the dim light of the crowded bazaar, it seems of an astounding brightness and spaciousness. The pavement is divided into squares by four pillars, and from these spring the arches of nine lofty domes, which are ornamented with elaborate arabesques and pierced by a number of small windows. On the sides of this great court, and also on a gallery above, are the offices of wholesale merchants and brokers, and at the rear are situated smaller courts and the vaulted storerooms of the khan. Around the central fountain between the pillars of the largest dome and crowding through the gateway and thronging the street outside, a vociferous throng of muleteers and camel-drivers are unloading the caravans which have come from Beirut on the coast and from northern Aleppo and across the desert from the Euphrates, bearing the choicest merchandise of the East, and some few machine-made products of the West, to swell "the riches of Damascus."[1]

There are real merchant-princes in this busy trading-center, and some of them live in royal splendor. The houses of the Damascus rich are truly palatial; but the stranger would never guess it from their exteriors, for the Syrian home has no elaborate façade and pretentious approach, such as the Franks delight to build. The prime object of the architect is to achieve the most absolute retirement for his patron. No window ever looks into that of a neighboring residence; no passer-by ever glimpses through an opened door the interior of a private dwelling. If the Englishman's house is his castle, the Syrian's is his retreat.

[1] Isaiah 8:4.

You pass along a dirty alley to an insignificant wooden door in a high stone wall. Just inside is the porter's cell; then comes a dark, vaulted passageway, which either has a sharp bend in it or else is screened at the farther end; then —

The open court which you enter may be three hundred feet across. Its tessellated pavement is of white marble inlaid with arabesques of darker stone. In the center is a fountain with designs of colored limestone set into its marble walls. Potted flowers bloom luxuriantly in the warm sunlight, and birds sing to the accompaniment of the splashing water. In the grateful shade of small fruit trees are placed bright rugs and soft cushions and tabarets made of rare woods inlaid with mother-of-pearl. The many lofty windows in the red and yellow striped walls of the surrounding dwelling are curtained with gorgeous silks.

At one side, usually the south, a spacious alcove reaches to the height of the second-story ceiling. This *liwân*, or drawing-room, is entirely open to the court; but its floor is raised a foot or two above the pavement outside, and its decorations are as rich and elaborate as if it were a huge, glittering jewel-box. No figures of men or animals are seen, for Moslems are forbidden to make representations of any living creature in the heavens above or the earth beneath or the waters under the earth;[2] yet it is

[2] According to the most strict Moslem teachers, the com-

Court and Liwân of a Damascus residence

Cemetery where members of Mohammed's family are buried

astonishing what splendid effects are evolved by their architects from the limited elements of Arabic script, geometric designs, foliage, fruits and flowers. In the *liwân* this arabesque ornamentation is profuse and elegant. The lower walls are built of alternate layers of differently colored stones, into which are set mosaic panels as intricate in design as the priceless rugs which lie upon the marble pavement. The woodwork of the room is all minutely carved, and inlaid with bits of glass and mother-of-pearl and sometimes even with jewels. The upper walls are frescoed in blue and green and gold, and from the gilded beams of the ceiling hang chandeliers of silver and beaten brass.

This half out-of-doors alcove gives access to the rooms which we should think of as being really in the house. Some of these may be even more lavishly decorated than the *liwân*, and all are comfortably furnished — according to the Syrian idea of comfort. Into the apartments of the ladies, however, no male guest may enter. These are *hareem* — "forbidden." Indeed, it is very likely that they are in a separate building, which opens on an inner court whose existence the casual visitor does not even suspect. No men save her nearest relatives are supposed ever to look upon the unveiled face of a Moslem woman. This prohibition, however, is of neces-

mandment of the Prophet (the *Koran,* sura 5:92, etc.) would prohibit the use of even the carved figures of the chess knights.

sity little observed among the poor, hard-working peasants and the desert Bedouins; and in the cities the universal characteristics of the female sex have not been entirely obliterated by the law of Islam. An unusually thin gauze almost always reveals a remarkably beautiful face, and I have seen veils coquettishly dropped — of course by accident — even in the bazaars of fanatical Damascus. Yet among the upper classes the thought of social intercourse between the sexes is so repellent that no good Moslem ever willingly alludes to his wife. If he is absolutely forced to speak of her, he apologizes by saying *Ajallak!* —“ May God lift you up! ”— that is, from the degradation of having to hear such a thing mentioned. He uses the identical expression when he refers to anything else unfit to be spoken of in conversation between gentlemen. “ Men are superior to women on account of the qualities with which God hath gifted the one above the other,” said the Prophet.[3] There is no place for female suffrage in the world of Islam!

If we think of Damascus as the port of the desert, then its wharves lie along the Meidan. This narrow handle of the spoon-shaped city, which stretches far southward on both sides of the *Derb el-Haj* or “ Pilgrim Road ” to Mecca, is a comparatively modern quarter; but it is most akin to the wilderness, and its one long avenue is thronged with Children

[3] The *Koran,* sura 4:38.

of the East who have journeyed far to visit what they firmly believe to be the world's largest and most beautiful city. Long caravans, weary, dusty and heavily laden, are led into the Meidan by wild-looking, shaggy Bedouins. A little flock of sheep on its way to the slaughter-house is driven by no gentle shepherd, but a black-bearded giant armed with rifle and dagger and club. Groaning camels kneel in the street while immense sacks of wheat are untied from their backs and rolled into the vaults of the grain-merchants. We see here the choicest mares of Arabia ridden by tall, stalwart Hauran Druses whose cruel, handsome faces, wrapped around with flowing headgears of spotless white, look down upon the hurrying crowds with a haughty contempt. Yonder group of strangely dressed fellows with red and white cloths bound about their brows are Chaldeans from Baghdad. The shops here seem very poor and shabby in comparison with the bazaars of the older quarters; but the simple country folk, and even the proud Bedouin Arabs, stand spellbound before the astounding wealth and bewildering tumult of the great city.

The south end of the Meidan is known as the Gate of Allah — though it has no gate; for it is here, amid impressive ceremonies, that there starts the annual Pilgrimage to Mecca.[4] Back to the same *Bab*

[4] In this effete generation, however, those who have the inclination and the money may take the sacred railway as far

Allah straggle, four months later, a sick and exhausted remnant who have survived the journey to the holy city, to bear henceforth the envied title of *haj* or "pilgrim." Then cholera or plague breaks out with renewed virulence.

Of the ancient fortifications of Damascus, only a short, ruinous piece now remains. The city is surrounded, between the houses and the orchards, by an almost unbroken succession of cemeteries. In the burying ground of the Orthodox Greeks is the small, unimpressive tomb of St. George, who is said to have assisted the Apostle Paul in his escape over the wall. This cannot, of course, be the same St. George who killed the dragon, as the hero of that famous exploit was not born until nearly three hundred years after the time of Paul.

In the large Moslem cemeteries at the southeast of the city are the tombs of Mohammed's muezzin, two of his nine wives, and his favorite child, Fatima. Not far from the sepulcher of the Prophet's daughter, though outside of the cemetery, is buried an unfortunate Jew who aspired to the hand of Fatima. The presumptuous lover is said to have been stoned to death, and his grave is now entirely hidden under a great heap of the rocks which pass-

as Medina, and for many years the majority of the pilgrims from outside of Syria have traveled by steamer to Jeddah, the seaport of Mecca — under the direction of an English tourist agency!

ing Moslems still cast upon it as a sign of their contempt.

Just outside of Damascus, also, is a sad house of "life more terrible than death." It was once, they say, the residence of proud Naaman, and it is still tenanted by lepers who, alas, have known no Elisha and washed in no healing Jordan. My Syrian friends were afraid even to enter its court, but I talked with eight of the thirty or forty inmates. Some were voiceless and shapeless — grotesque, horrible caricatures of humanity. But there was still a "little maid" in the House of Naaman. Miriam was a pretty, slender girl, just beginning to burst into the bloom of early Eastern adolescence. She seemed the very incarnation of health and youthful joy, and could hardly stop laughing long enough for me to take her photograph. Yet I could not laugh with her; for on the rich brown of her cheek was a tiny pinkish swelling, and close beside her graceful form crouched an awful figure, loathsome, unsmiling and unwomanly, like which she would some day be.

Over the now closed Kisan Gate at the southeast corner of the city wall is a small, bricked-up window, through which tradition says that St. Paul was let down in a basket. Unfortunately for the story, this part of the fortification dates from the Turkish occupation. The bend of the wall includes, however, as it probably has always done, the Jewish Quarter.

The Hebrews of Damascus are unique among their coreligionists of Palestine and Syria in that they are not comparatively recent immigrants drawn back to the land of their fathers by Zionist ideals, but are descended from ancestors who settled here in very ancient times.[5] Some of them bear family names which can be read in the earliest census lists of the Old Testament. Many of them are very estimable people; but I cannot describe the quarter where they live, further than to state that it is the most filthy and malodorous place I have yet visited. I am not especially squeamish; I have often, for the sake of the human interest found there, traveled in Mediterranean steerages and lived in the slums of great capitals; but after a brief glimpse of the Jewish Quarter of Damascus, I beat an ignominious retreat. There are said to be houses there whose interiors are wonderfully beautiful; but I am not going back to see them.

There are in all five "quarters" in Damascus: the Christian and the Jewish at the east, the peasant market of the Meidan at the south, the suburb of el-Amara north of the Barada, and the Moslem heart of the city. The "Street called Straight,"[6] which

[5] See further the author's *The Real Palestine of To-day*, chapter VII.

[6] Acts 9:11. The ancient name has survived, or possibly has been revived, and the thoroughfare is still called *Derb el-Mustakîm* or "Straight Street." Its more common name, however, is *Suk et-Tawîleh,* the "Long Bazaar."

cuts across the center of the bazaar district from east to west, may roughly be considered the dividing line between the Jewish and the Christian Quarters. The flippant jest to the effect that the writer of the Acts said only that the thoroughfare was "called" straight, is hardly justified by the facts. This is, in fact, the straightest, longest street in all Damascus, as well as one of the widest. It was once divided into three parallel roadways by Corinthian colonnades, some few remains of which can still be found. To-day it is covered for half its length with a high, arching metal roof, and contains many of the largest and most modern stores in the city.

Beside this busy bazaar the Damascus Moslems show the tomb of the disciple Ananias, whose memory they hold in great respect. His reputed residence, which lies some distance away in the center of the Christian Quarter, is in charge of Latin monks. All that remains of the house is a low, cave-like chapel, twenty or more feet below the street. By itself, however, this fact furnishes no argument against the correctness of the location; for the level of every crumbling, undrained Syrian city constantly rises century by century.

Turning now into the Moslem Quarter, we pass through a tasteful little garden, closely planted with shade trees, and enter an unpretentious building. Here rests one of the greatest Moslem heroes and the most formidable opponent of the Crusaders —

the invincible Salah ed-Din, whose sonorous name we Franks pronounce "Saladin." It seems very strange that the tomb of this valiant champion of Islam was long unhonored, if not entirely unknown, by the inhabitants of Damascus, until it was discovered fifty years ago by an American missionary. The original casket of walnut has since been replaced by an exquisitely carved marble sarcophagus, upon which lies a cover of green silk. In a niche of the wall at the foot of the tomb now hangs the large bronze wreath given by the German Emperor in memory of his visit to Damascus. One hopes that it was a Christian spirit of forgiveness which prompted the placing of a Maltese cross on this tribute to the Crusaders' greatest foeman. But as soon as the Christian emblem was noticed by the custodian of the tomb, the wreath was removed from its original position on the sarcophagus.

The one notable ancient building in Damascus is the great mosque of *Neby Yahya* or "St. John," better known to the Western world as the Omayyade Mosque. The site where this stands has probably always been marked by a place of worship, and the present structure is some of those immemorial religious edifices which, so far as we definitely know, was never built, but only rebuilt. It was doubtless here that there stood the House of Rimmon in which Naaman, captain of the host of the king of Syria,

The street called Straight

The Bride's Minaret of the Omayyade Mosque

bowed down with his royal master.[7] About the year 400 A. D. the then Roman temple was transformed into the Church of St. John the Baptist. When Damascus fell into the hands of the Omayyade Dynasty in the seventh century, the Christian house of worship was converted into a mosque of such miraculous splendor that the vast multitude of human artists and artisans who labored upon it were later believed to have been assisted by the genii. All Syria was ransacked for ancient columns to adorn the new structure. The pavement was of the most expensive marbles, the prayer-niches and pulpits were set with jewels, the carved wooden ceiling was inlaid with precious metals, and six hundred hanging lamps of solid gold cast their mellow light upon the exquisite mosaic decorations. Since then, the building has been burned and burned again, and at each restoration has lost something of its former magnificence. Yet still it ranks with St. Sophia of Constantinople, the Dome of the Rock at Jerusalem and the Sacred Mosque of Mecca, as one of the greatest of Moslem sanctuaries.

Time would fail to tell of its size and splendor, its holy impressiveness to Moslem eyes, and the inspiring views from its lofty minarets. In its great court rise the Dome of the Hours and the Dome of the Fountain, which is believed to mark a point on

[7] II Kings 5:18.

the Pilgrim Route exactly half-way between Constantinople and Mecca, and the Dome of the Treasure, where, hidden jealously from infidel eyes, are kept the sacred books and the records of the mosque. Above tower three minarets, which are known as the Western, the Bride's and — strange as this name may at first seem — the Minaret of Jesus. The Moslems, however, believe that 'Isa, as they call Him, was one of the greatest of the prophets, hardly, if at all, inferior to Mohammed himself;[8] and the "Son of Mary" is held in unusual reverence by the inhabitants of Damascus, who say that He will stand upon this minaret at the Last Judgment.

The mosque itself extends along the entire southern side of the court. I know of no other non-Gothic structure which seems so well fitted to uplift one's thoughts in solemn, spiritual worship of the unseen

[8] Jesus is frequently mentioned in the Koran as a prophet, though His divinity is denied and the Christian Trinity is misunderstood by Mohammed as consisting of the Father, Son and Virgin Mary. Characteristic passages are: "O Mary! Verily God announces to thee the Word from Him: his name shall be Messiah Jesus the Son of Mary, illustrious in this world and in the next, and one of those who have near access to God. And He will teach him the Book, and the Wisdom, and the Law, and the Evangel, and he shall be an apostle to the Children of Israel" (Sura 3:40, 43). But—"It beseemeth not God to beget a son" (Sura 19:36). "God shall say, O Jesus, Son of Mary, hast thou said unto mankind, Take me and my mother as two gods, besides God?" (Sura 5:116). "Jesus is no more than a servant whom We favored" (Sura 43:59).

God. Here are no confusing chapels, no gaudy pictures or distracting statues, no gilded altar lit by smoking candles, no thin blue clouds of slowly rising incense. All is clean, bright, commodious, and yet of an appropriate richness and beauty. A careful inspection shows that the architects used the ground-plan of a basilica with aisles and transepts; but, in spite of the two rows of columns and the heavier pillars which support the central "Dome of the Eagle," the chief and lasting impression of the mosque is its ample, unbroken spaciousness.

The building is larger even than the visitor first thinks: a hundred and fifty paces will hardly take him from one end of it to the other. Its stone floor is entirely covered by rugs, whose variegated patterns have worn to a dull, somber tint. From the lofty ceiling a multitude of lamps and several gigantic chandeliers are hung by long chains, so low that they just clear the head of a tall man. Between two of the columns stands a lavishly decorated, domed structure which is said to contain the head of John the Baptist, after whom the mosque is named. The shrine is about the size of the Chapel of the Sepulcher at Jerusalem, but it seems smaller on account of the far larger building which surrounds it. In the south wall of the mosque — toward Mecca — are four shallow prayer-niches, and near the middle of this side stands a tall, graceful pulpit, whose minute and elaborate inlays of silver and ivory and mother-of-pearl make it a marvel of chaste richness. Unlike all Oriental churches and most other mosques, there is comparatively little gold used in the decoration of this great building. The prevailing colors are cool white and blue and silver, and the really immense amount of mosaic and inlaid work seems hardly more than delicate tracery upon the broad, unbroken surfaces.

Such is the Great Mosque when it is empty, a fitting place for quiet communion and solemn contemplation of the vastness and unhurried power of the Almighty. But when you behold this same building thronged with strangely garbed, proud, intellectual-looking and intensely devout men — women are seldom seen in mosques — you feel the grip of something portentous, irresistible, relentless. Long lines of turbaned figures facing toward the holy city of Arabia, now bending low together like a field of wheat swept by the summer breeze, now standing erect with arms outstretched toward Allah the Merciful and Compassionate, reciting their confession of faith in shrill, quick tones which lose their individuality in a tremendous momentum of sound like the wave-beat of the sea — these thousands of worshipers have firm hold on a great truth, though it be but a half-truth; they believe in their religion with an impregnable, unquestioning confidence, and they render to its precepts an implicit obedience such as is not enforced by any Christian sect in the world. They would gladly die for the faith of Islam, and nothing but the strong restraint of European armaments holds them back from again raising the standard of the Prophet and setting forth on a new *jahâd,* or holy war, in obedience to the sacred mandate, "When ye encounter the unbelievers, strike off their heads until ye have made a great slaughter among them. . . . As for the infidels, let them perish, and their works shall God bring to nought. . . . And their dwelling the hell fire! . . . Be not faint hearted then, and invite not the infidels to peace!"[9]

Be he preacher or statesman, that man is a fool and blind who does not realize the tremendous vitality and undiminished strength of Mohammedanism, the power instinct in its half-truths, and the unsleeping menace of its essential antagonism to all the "infidel" world. Politically, Islam is being rapidly shorn of its power; but as a religion — a religion for which men will cheerfully give their lives — it has lost no whit of its potency. As the cry of the muezzin echoes across the earth to-day from Japan to Gibraltar, there are, not fewer, but many millions more who obey its call than there were four centuries ago when Mohammed II. hurled his Turkish regiments against the ramparts of a then Christian Constantinople.

The Omayyade Mosque, as has been said, was once

[9] The *Koran,* sura 47:4, 9, 13, 37.

a church. In the marble wall beside its most beautiful prayer-niche is set a large mosaic panel, among whose intricate geometric traceries there stand out distinctly three large Maltese crosses. The Moslem artist apparently copied the design from some earlier decoration without realizing that he was including the hated symbol of Christianity. So the worshipers in the Great Mosque who face towards Mecca face also the Cross!

But the strangest feature of this ancient sanctuary is seldom viewed by travelers; for it is hard to reach, and dragomans are averse to taking the necessary trouble. You must go to the Joiners' Bazaar, which lies just south of the mosque, and borrow a long ladder. Setting this up in the busy street, you then climb through a small hole which has been broken in the wall just under the roof of the covered bazaar, and step out upon a dusty housetop. Here is seen a bit of an old stone portal, elaborately carved with leaves and flowers, and bearing on its lintel the unexpected Greek inscription, standing out clearly in capital letters —

THY KINGDOM, O CHRIST, IS AN EVERLASTING KINGDOM,
AND THY DOMINION ENDURETH THROUGHOUT ALL GENERATIONS.

It is a startling, suggestive sentence to read upon

the wall of the greatest mosque of fanatical Moslem Damascus. But you have to get up on the house-tops before you can read the promise that is written there.

CHAPTER X

THE DESERT CAPITAL

JUST half-way along the ancient caravan route which runs northeast from Damascus to the Euphrates River are the ruins of one of the most remarkable cities of history; for here, in the midst of the desert, Palmyra attained a wonderful degree of wealth and culture, and a military power which for a time rivaled that of Rome itself.

The road thither is nearly always in the desert. This is not, however, a level waste of sand; on the contrary, it is often quite a hilly country, where for hours at a time the traveler passes along narrow valleys between steep, rugged heights. The trail has been beaten so hard by the tread of innumerable caravans that one could ride all the way to Palmyra on a bicycle. In fact, tourist agents used sometimes to take parties there by automobile. But this practice was soon abandoned, because break-downs were frequent, and there were no garages where repairs might be made. Our own party traveled on horseback, with the heavy luggage carried by several donkeys and one very lively pack-camel who took advantage of every possible opportunity to run away across the desert.

However you may go to Palmyra, it is not an easy journey. In summer the sun is fearfully hot, and in winter the wilderness wind is piercingly cold; the water along the route, while perhaps not actually unhealthful, is warm and evil-tasting and full of animal life; unless you carry your own tent you must sleep in hovels which are filthy and insect-ridden, and marauding bands of Bedouins hover about, watching for a chance to rob the luckless traveler.

Two days' journey from Damascus, near the ancient and now very squalid village of Karyatein, are a number of ruins which date from Græco-Roman times. One of these, an extensive sanitarium, is known as the "Bath of Balkis"— the traditional name of the Queen of Sheba. Within the enclosure is a vaulted room with a paved floor, in the middle of which an opening some ten inches in diameter sends forth a current of moist, hot, sulphurous air. The heat of this room was so suffocating that we could endure it only for a moment; but the air is believed to be beneficial for certain diseases, and in Roman days the place was very popular as a health resort.

From Karyatein the trail strikes across a broad plain between two mountain ranges. This plain is about fifty miles, or eighteen camel-hours, long, and its springs are very few and very poor. The Syrian Desert shows no vegetation in summer except a low salsolaceous thorn-bush, which the Arabs burn for its soda ash. This plant is called *al-kali*, whence comes our word "alkali." It was formerly extensively used in the manufacture of soap; but on account of the importation of cheaper materials it no longer has any commercial value.

In the middle of the day the heat was intense. Our heads were protected from the direct rays of the sun by thick pith helmets, but the reflection of the cloudless sky upon the whitish marl of the plain scorched our faces and the flies were a torment to all except the camel, whose thick hide seemed proof against their attacks.

We had planned to replenish our canteens at Ain el-Wu'ul; but the wells there proved to be choked with locusts, and at Ain el-Beida, which we reached after fourteen hours in the saddle, we found the water so strongly impregnated with sulphur that it tasted like a dose of warm medicine. This was the last spring in the district, however, so we had no choice but to drink the nauseating stuff.

A small garrison of Turkish soldiers was stationed in this out-of-the-way place to protect caravans against the Bedouins, who roam the desert in the hope of plundering unwary travelers. These robber tribes view their nefarious occupation as a legitimate business, a feature of desert life which has become, so to speak, legalized by immemorial custom.

They regard the traveler exactly as the hunter does his prey — a bounty sent by Providence, which it would be ungrateful for them not to accept. They will strip their victim to the skin, but are careful not to take his life unless resistance is offered. They leave him naked in the wilderness under the protection of Allah, who must take the responsibility, should the poor fellow perish from hunger and thirst and exposure.

Early the next morning we saw a band of such Arab raiders passing across the plain a few miles west of us, and all day we proceeded with the greatest caution, for fear they might swoop down upon us. We afterwards learned that their last foray had been unsuccessful, and consequently they were returning to their encampment in an unamiable frame of mind which would have boded ill to us if we had happened to cross their path.

Midway between Ain el-Beida and Palmyra, we made a détour to visit some mountains a little distance to the left of the trail. We found here two altars about six feet high, bearing bi-lingual inscriptions in Greek and Palmyrene, which related that they had been erected on March 21 of the year of Palmyra 425 (114 A. D.), and were dedicated to the "Most High God." Near by could be seen the broken base of a third monument, but there were no other indications of human handiwork. We concluded that these altars must mark the course of the ancient highway, which the city was under obligation to maintain and protect.

The hills on either side of the plain now drew very much nearer to us and, as we approached the narrow pass which leads to the desert city, we saw beside the road several strange mortuary towers. These are as characteristic a feature of the environs of Palmyra as are the tombs on the Appian Way of the approach to Rome. Several of the structures are in a fair state of preservation and show clearly the original form and use. They were each of three or four stories, the upper floors being reached by inside stairways. Each story consisted of one square room surrounded by *loculi* for the reception of the dead, and before these, or standing within the room, were statues of the persons entombed in the niches. The statues either have been badly mutilated by the Arabs, who have a religious aversion to all such "idolatrous" representations, or have been destroyed by the vandalism of ignorant dealers in antiquities who, when they found it inconvenient to carry off whole figures, would break them and smuggle away the fragments. Many such heads, arms and feet have found their way to the coast cities of Syria, and some few have been sold to European palaces and museums.

Our long journey down the pass ended at a low saddle between the hills, and we at last looked down upon Palmyra itself. Just below us stretched a vast, confused mass of broken, reddish stones, from which rose here and there a group of graceful columns or the massive wall of a ruined temple. Back of the city were the desert hills; before it lay the desert plain. Built by a spring at the crossroads of the wilderness — surely no other of the world's great capitals had so strange a site as this one!

The thrilling story of Palmyra's rise and fall has been enshrined in poetry and romance and has inspired the painter's genius. The city lay, as has been said, midway between Damascus and the Euphrates, on the most fertile oasis along the ancient caravan route. It thus early became the center of the trade between the Mediterranean countries and the heart of western Asia. If, as is probable, the Tadmor or Tamar (Palm City) of the Bible [1] is the same as Palmyra, then it was built (or, more probably, rebuilt) by Solomon; but it does not again emerge into historical notice until about the beginning of the Christian era, when Mark Antony led an unsuccessful expedition against it. Still later, the Roman emperors recognized Palmyra as an important ally and buffer-state against the inroads of the Parthians. In the third century the Empire was thrown into a state of anarchy by continual contests between rival claimants for the throne; so, though in theory distant Palmyra was only a "col-

[1] I Kings 9:18.

ony," it was in fact given, or better, allowed to assume, a practical independence. Its ruler Odenathus II. bore the title of Augustus, which was inferior only to that of Emperor. After his death he was known as the "King of kings." In reality, he was the absolute ruler of a sovereign state.

When Valerian had been put to rout by Sapor of Persia, it was Odenathus who decisively defeated the invaders, saved the Roman Empire from what seemed certain overthrow, and incidentally added Mesopotamia to his own royal domains. This king of Palmyra would doubtless have proved a formidable rival of the emperor, had not his life been cut short by assassination in the year 266.

Odenathus was succeeded by his son Vahballathus; but the real ruler was his widow Bath Zebina, better known to the Western world by the Greek form of her name, Zenobia. If we consider her intellectual power, administrative ability and personal character, Zenobia ranks as one of the greatest, if not the greatest, of all queens. She was as gifted in military affairs as Semiramis, as strong a ruler as Elizabeth, as beautiful as her ancestor Cleopatra, more learned than Catherine, and her private life was never touched by the breath of calumny.

She is described as of surpassing loveliness, according to the Oriental type of beauty, with sparkling black eyes, pearly teeth and a commanding presence. She spoke Greek and Coptic fluently and knew

A few of the ruins which crowd the site of ancient Palmyra

The Triple Gate and the Temple of the Sun

some Latin, in addition, of course, to her native Aramean. She drew up for her own use an epitome of history, delighted in reading Homer and Plato, and beguiled her leisure by discussing philosophy with the famous scholar Longinus, whom she persuaded to take up a permanent residence at her court.

Her physical endurance was remarkable. While her husband was living, she was accustomed to accompany him on his hunting expeditions. After the death of Odenathus, she habitually rode at the head of her armies on a fiery stallion, from which, however, she would often dismount, so that she might share the fatigue of the march with the common soldiers. It is no wonder that such a leader —beautiful, pure, brave, queenly yet friendly — inspired in her armies an intense personal loyalty and an unquestioning assent to her most daring plans. Without a murmur they followed their beloved queen into the fearful struggle with the world-empire.

At the very beginning of her reign, she threw down the gauntlet to Rome. The sway of Palmyra already extended over Armenia and Mesopotamia. An army of 70,000 men now defeated the Roman legions by the Nile and annexed Egypt. Zenobia next pushed her victorious banners northward to the very shores of the Bosphorus. When the newly elected emperor Aurelian insisted that she should formally acknowledge his sovereignty, her answer was a bold defiance and a proclamation of herself and her son as supreme rulers of the whole East.

Aurelian, however, was of different stuff from his weakling predecessors. In the year 272 he brought an immense army to Syria, defeated the forces of Zenobia at Antioch and then, following quickly after the retreating Palmyrenes, routed them again near the city of Emesa (modern Homs) and demanded of Zenobia that she surrender. The haughty answer was that her enemy had not yet even begun to test the valor and resources of Palmyra.

So the great army of Rome laid siege to the desert stronghold. The winter and spring wore on, and Zenobia was still unconquered. Whenever Aurelian summoned her to capitulate, she responded with another bold defiance. But at last it became clear that her capital was doomed; so the queen, escaping the vigilance of the Roman sentries, slipped away from the city and fled across the desert toward the Euphrates. Just as she reached the bank of the river, however, she was overtaken and brought back captive. Yet her proud spirit remained unbroken. When Aurelian reproached her for her obstinate and useless rebellion, she answered with calm dignity that the course of events had indeed proved his supremacy, but that the previous emperors had not shown themselves to be superior to her, and she had therefore been justified in opposing their authority.

In spite of the stubborn resistance of the city, Aurelian did not now destroy Palmyra or treat its inhabitants cruelly. But when he reached the Bosphorus on his way back to Rome, word came that the Palmyrenes had already revolted and had slain the Roman garrison left by the conqueror. Thereupon he quickly retraced his march and recaptured the city without difficulty. This time the enraged emperor ordered the beautiful capital to be razed and allowed his soldiers to engage in an awful massacre. Neither women nor children were spared, and when the avenging army finally left the unhappy city, its splendid buildings were but heaps of dusty rubbish, among which hid a miserable remnant of its heartbroken inhabitants. Thus departed forever the glory of Palmyra.

The heart of the world has been touched by the pathetic spectacle of proud, beautiful Zenobia led captive through the streets of Rome to grace Aurelian's triumphal procession. Yet the emperor seems to have treated his captive with unusual consideration and respect, and he generously bestowed upon her a large estate near Tivoli. There, in the company of her two sons, she passed the rest of her days quietly, though we dare not hope happily.

Palmyra was afterwards partially rebuilt by Diocletian and was fortified by Justinian, who made it a garrison town; but it never regained its former prosperity. The city was overrun by the desert Arabs, and suffered severely during the conflicts among the rival Moslem conquerors of Syria. In the year 745 it was again destroyed; in the eleventh and twelfth centuries it suffered from severe earthquakes; in 1401 it was plundered by the Tartar Tamerlane; in the sixteenth century it was taken by the Druses, and in the seventeenth it was razed by the Turks. For many generations the ancient city on the oasis was completely unknown to the Western world, though the wandering Bedouins delighted to talk of the marvelous ruins in the midst of the great desert.

Modern Tadmor — for it has taken again its old Semitic name — is but a wretched Arab hamlet of perhaps three hundred inhabitants, whose mud-plastered hovels lie in the midst of imposing ruins. Fully a square mile of the plain is strewn with the débris of temples, palaces and majestic colonnades. Many columns are still standing, after having braved the wars and earthquakes of sixteen centuries; but by far the greater number of them lie prone on the ground, half buried by the drifting dust.

The most prominent object that meets the eye is the Great Temple of Baal, the sun-god, which stands on a high platform overlooking the plain. Although Aurelian himself had this edifice restored after the final subjugation of Palmyra, it has since been badly damaged by earthquakes and defaced by the fanaticism of Moslem iconoclasts. Yet eight of its tall fluted columns and practically all of one side-wall enable us to guess what must have been the beauty of this structure when it was the chief sanctuary of Zenobia's capital.

Other ruins rise above the intricate mass of fallen columns which cover the area occupied by the ancient city. This huge pile of carved stones surmounted by a broken portico was once the royal palace. Yonder curving colonnade includes the fragments of the theater. Smaller temples are recognized here and there, and on the hillside at the edge of the oasis can be seen a number of the tall, square towers which were built as burial-places for the wealthier families.

But the chief architectural glory of ancient Palmyra was its far-famed Street of Columns. This imposing avenue stretched from the western edge of the oasis to the Temple of the Sun, a distance of about three-quarters of a mile. On each side of it was a continuous, elaborately carved entablature, supported by nearly four hundred columns of reddish-brown limestone. About two-thirds of the way up these columns were corbels which, as the inscriptions still show, bore statues of prominent citizens. At every important crossing, whence other colonnaded avenues stretched to the right and left, four massive granite pillars supported a vaulted *tetrapylon* or quadruple gate.

Over a hundred of the columns of this beautiful avenue are still standing in their places, and large portions of the entablature remain unbroken. One can easily follow the course of the colonnade and understand its relation to adjoining structures; and the traveler must be sadly lacking in imagination who cannot sometimes, as the light of the twentieth century day grows dimmer, see a dream city of wondrous, unbroken beauty stand proud again beneath the calm, still gleaming of the desert stars. Not shattered stones but well-built homes and busy bazaars spread far outward from the foot of the mountain; a multitude of graceful pillars stand upright around the palaces and temples of a mighty capital, and between the long lines of statues on the reddish shafts of the great colonnade a splendid vista reaches to the triumphal arch and then, through its triple portals, to where the Temple of the Sun keeps silent watch over a city of imperial grandeur and a queen who sees visions of world-wide dominion.

The few hundred residents of Tadmor are of Arab blood, but the Bedouins of the surrounding desert consider them a poor, degenerate race, as doubtless they are. Shortly before we visited the village, its sheikh had made a wonderful trip to Paris as guest of a French lady who had previously traveled through the desert under his guidance. It seemed very strange, in this lonely little hamlet among the ruins of a vanished people, to hear an Arab sheikh tell stories — and he loved to tell them — about his adventures in the most modern of twentieth century capitals.

We were so fortunate as to be invited to a great

feast which the sheikh gave the entire village in honor of his birthday. Feeding the poor in this wholesale way is regarded by the Arabs as a deed of great merit. A slaughtered camel provided the *pièce de résistance* of the banquet. In the center of the room was placed an enormous tray piled with a mountain of *burghul*, or boiled wheat, into which had been inserted huge pieces of camel's meat. A large funnel-shaped depression had been scooped out in the top of the pile and filled with melted butter. This percolated through the mass and added the final touch of flavor to what was — if you liked it — a most rich and delicious repast. The anxious villagers were then admitted in groups of eight or ten. They immediately squatted around the tray, thrust their hands into the mass, grasped as much as they could, plunged it into their mouths and, in order not to lose any time, swallowed it with as little mastication as possible. One greedy fellow got an unusually large chunk of camel's meat into his throat and, as a consequence, nearly choked to death before his comrades relieved him by strenuous blows upon his back.

In order to visit Hama, we returned from Palmyra by another route; and, as a large part of this journey was to be across a trackless, waterless and absolutely uninhabited desert, we engaged a Bedouin to act as our guide.

Not long after setting out, we passed through a gap in the hills a quarter of a mile wide, whose sides were almost as perpendicular as if they had been walls shaped by the hand of man. The locality is called *Marbat Antar*, that is, "Antar's Hitching-place." Antar is the hero of many a fabulous exploit among the Arabs, much as was Hercules among the Greeks; and the prodigies of valor which he performed in defense of his tribe are celebrated in song and story. Among other wonderful feats, he is said to have leaped his horse across this deep ravine from cliff to cliff.

The first day's journey homeward brought us to el-Wesen, a well where we had expected to lay in a supply of water for the long ride across the arid wilderness; but, to our intense disappointment, we found the water foul with dead locusts. Our Arabs, however, swallowed the nauseating fluid with great gusto, apparently rejoicing that they could obtain both food and drink in the same mouthful; and, as it was a case of necessity, we managed to cook some food with the water, and even drank a little of it in the form of very strong tea which disguised somewhat the insect flavor.

The next morning we were ready for the start at four o'clock and traveled all day through a rolling, treeless country, which in summer is absolutely bare of vegetation. At sunset we halted for two hours in order to rest and feed the animals. Then we mounted again for an all-night ride; for we did not dare sleep until we had come to water. There was no trail visible to us, but our guide held steadily on through the darkness. During the long night we could see ahead of us his white camel, keeping straight on the course with no apparent aid save the twinkling stars above. There was such danger of falling in with one of the robber tribes which infest this district that we were warned not to speak above a whisper. The poor donkeys also received a hint not to bray. Each of them had a halter looped tightly around his neck. As soon as an animal was seen to raise his nose in preparation for an ecstatic song, some one would quickly tighten the noose and, to our amusement and the donkey's very evident disgust, the only sound to issue from his throat would be a thin gurgling whine.

As the night drew on we became so sleepy that we could hardly sit in the saddles, and before morning dawned we were burning with thirst. Our guide led us to another spring. Not only was it full of long-dead locusts, but a wild pig was wallowing in the filthy water! Even the Arabs refused to drink from the pool that had been defiled by the unclean beast. There was nothing to do but to push on again. We had been twenty-six hours in the saddle, with nothing to drink save "locust-tea," when at last we came to a little village by a running stream of clear, limpid water — and our desert journey was safely over.

CHAPTER XI

SOME SALT PEOPLE

WHENEVER the genial American consul-general spoke of a certain godly Scotch-woman who was laboring for the uplift of Syria, a not irreverent twinkle would come into his eye as he paraphrased the words of the Gospel — "She is one of those salt people."

I should like to write a book about the men and women of many races and many ecclesiastical affiliations whose lives are bringing a varied savor and moral asepsis to the land of Syria. It would contain tales of thrilling romance and brave adventure and a surprising number of humorous anecdotes, besides the record of quiet self-devotion which is taken for granted in all missionary biographies. Such a lengthy narration falls without the scope of the present work. Yet any description of Syria and its people would be incomplete which did not include at least a few glimpses of the men and women who, more than all others, are molding the thought and uplifting the ideals and helping to solve the critical problems of the land of Lebanon.

Earnest faith, noble character and uncomplaining self-sacrifice are not sufficient equipment for the Syrian missionary. These qualities are indeed needed, and as a rule are possessed in generous measure. But he who is to exert any permanent influence for good upon this proud, sturdy, persistent, quick-witted race, with its almost cynical proficiency in religious argumentation, must also be strong of body, alert of intellect, tactful in social intercourse, and withal of an adaptability born not of vacillation but of a firm hold on the essentials of life.

Among the American missionaries, for instance, have been found champion athletes, splendid riders and marksmen, *raconteurs* of surprising mental agility, phenomenal linguists and surgeons of magnificent daring. One gained world-wide fame as an author and another as a scientist. A third was the best Arabic scholar of his century, if not of any century. Well-known American colleges have called — in vain — for presidents from Syria; and an important embassy of the United States was thrice offered to a missionary, who preferred, however, to keep to his chosen life-work — at eight hundred dollars a year. These men and women are not laboring here because there is no other field of endeavor open to them. They are very intelligent, competent, refined, brave, adaptable people, with deep knowledge of many other things besides religion, a broad vision of the world's affairs, and almost invariably a keen sense of humor;

people whom it is an education to know and a glad inspiration to own as friends.

In 1855 a leaky sailing vessel landed a cargo of rum and missionaries at Beirut. The rum was drunk up long ago; but one of the passengers, a tall, wiry Yankee, is still bubbling over with the joy of life. When I met Dr. Bliss again in Syria last summer, he told me with quiet chuckles of enjoyment how, shortly after he came to the East, one of the older missionaries remarked, "Daniel Bliss isn't practical and his wife won't live a year in this climate." After nearly sixty years, the beloved wife is still with him; and as for being practical — there stands the great university which he has built!

Others helped him from the beginning — wise and generous philanthropists like William E. Dodge and Morris K. Jesup in America and the Duke of Argyll and the Earl of Shaftesbury in Great Britain — but two thousand alumni scattered over the five continents will tell you that the Syrian Protestant College is first and foremost a monument to the foresight and tact and self-sacrifice and patience and indomitable enthusiasm of "the Old Doctor."

It was at first very small. A half-century ago there were but a few pupils gathered in a hired room. To-day the faculty and administrative officers alone number nearly four score, and a thousand men and boys are studying *in the English language*. The institution is emphatically Christian, but it is as absolutely non-sectarian as Harvard or Columbia. Every great religion and sect of the Near East, including Mohammedanism and Judaism, is represented in the student body; and it is hardly an exaggeration to say that every student and graduate honors Daniel Bliss next only to God. As he walks through the streets of the city, men stop to kiss his hands — which embarrasses him exceedingly. Perhaps they love him so much because they are so sure that he loves them. Orientals are very quick to detect a stranger's underlying motives, and many a smooth-speaking philanthropist has been weighed by them and found wanting. But, during nearly sixty years' residence in Beirut, Dr. Bliss has lived such a life that his devotion to Syria and his affectionate interest in Syrians has become a tradition handed down from father to son.

He has known dark days and fought hard battles, yet he has never lacked a buoyant optimism, born partly of trust in God and partly of a strong body and a healthful mind. He has no patience with dismal, despondent prophets of evil. I never knew a man with a larger capacity for enjoyment. Good music always moves him powerfully. He keeps in touch with the latest European and American periodicals. He likes new books, new songs, new stories and, especially, new jokes. Active, alert, quick at repartee, he is passionately fond of the society of young people, and they repay the liking with interest.

A visitor to the college was once speaking of the attractive horseback rides through the country around Beirut. "But," he added, as he looked up at the white-haired president, "I suppose you don't ride any more." "No," answered Dr. Bliss with a resigned sigh, "I haven't been on a horse for — three days!"

He is getting on in years now, and a recent stoop has taken a fraction of an inch from his six feet of spare, hard bone and muscle. A decade ago he resigned the presidency of the college, whereupon, to his great delight, his son was elected to fill the vacancy. "See what my boy is doing!" he exclaims, as he shows visitors the new buildings which are going up almost at the rate of one a year. So now the Old Doctor just walks about the campus which he loves, and from beneath his shock of thick white hair beams an irresistibly infectious enjoyment of this superlatively beautiful world, where anybody who has the mind can work so hard and get so much fun out of it.

Did I say that Dr. Bliss is old? Not he! He would indignantly deny the imputation. It is true that he celebrated his ninetieth birthday last August, but what of that? He recently expressed an intention to live to be a hundred. When he was a stalwart youth of four score I heard him remark, "Let the aged people talk about the good old times if they want to. I have no patience with such old fogies. *I* believe that the world is getting better every day."

Ras Baalbek is a little village some twenty miles north of the famous temples. Its thousand inhabitants are exceedingly ignorant and bigoted Oriental Catholics. The only native Protestant family is that of the school-teacher. There is also one American citizen — an adopted brother of ours who accumulated a few hundred dollars in the United States, learned a few words of English, and then returned to his birthplace, where he keeps the village khan, which has an evil reputation as a gambling-house. The Ras is cold in winter, hot in summer, and filthy at all seasons. The houses are built half of mud and half of stone; the streets are filled with unmitigated mud. A legion of fierce curs fill the night with their howling, and rush out of dark corners to snap at unsuspecting strangers.

It was not an inviting town, but we had heard that two American ladies were spending the winter there in missionary work; so, after we had turned over our horses to our fellow citizen of the khan and had dug passably clean collars out of our dusty saddle-bags, we went to pay them an evening call. Their house was not hard to find, for it was the finest in all the village, a commodious mansion with two rooms, one built of stone and the other of mud.

When the door opened for us, we passed immediately from Syria to America and, under the influence of the warmth and refinement and hospitable cheer of the mud-walled room, our sentiments toward Ras Baalbek underwent a complete and permanent change. These quiet-speaking, refined ladies did not look at all like martyrs of the faith. It was hard to realize that they had immured themselves in the midst of a dirty, ignorant, fanatical community, and were living in circumstances of very real hardship and peril. In the street just outside, the dogs were yelping noisily. From a neighboring roof a stentorian voice called out what corresponded to the evening edition of a local newspaper. The village was informed that the robber-tribe of Beit Dendish was ravaging the valley, a prominent resident had been murdered the preceding night, and Abu somebody-or-other had lost one of his goats. In the bright, warm room, however, we talked of American friends and American books, and discussed the probable outcome of the Yale-Princeton game.

After supper we all went to the house of the native teacher for a little prayer meeting. He was a young married man with several children, but his housekeeping arrangements were very simple. There was but one room. The floor was of mud, the ceiling was mud and straw, the walls were mud and stone. In one corner was a big pile of mattresses and blankets; in another was a small pile of cooking utensils, and one wall was hollowed out to serve as a bin for flour. The teacher's children lay on mattresses spread upon the bare floor and slept quite soundly through all the talking and singing.

As there were no other Protestants in the village, the attendance was naturally small. Two or three neighbors slipped in quietly and seated themselves by the door. These Catholics were probably drawn here merely by curiosity to see the American ladies and their visitors; but they sat reverently through the service and seemed to pay very close attention, though their dark, inscrutable faces gave no hint as to what they thought of the proceedings.

It was not an inspiring audience; but the ladies met each newcomer with a bright smile and a tactful word of greeting. We sang strange-sounding words to an old, familiar tune, after which one of the missionaries read a few verses from the Bible and added a brief explanation of their meaning. The second hymn was set to an Arab air that sounded a little startling to our Western ears. Then came a short closing prayer, followed immediately by very lengthy Oriental salutations, as the two strangers were introduced to the people of the Ras.

We should have liked to stay several days and investigate at first-hand the work among women, of which we had heard encouraging reports; but we had to ride away early the next morning. The two missionaries walked out to the edge of the village with us, where the older lady gave us a ridiculously large lunch and a pleasant invitation to "call again the next time you are passing!" The younger — she was very young — pretended to weep copiously at our departure, and wrung bucketfuls of imaginary tears out of her handkerchief. Then the two cheery figures went back up the hill to their long, lonely winter of exile.

On the last Sunday of the Old Year the air was just crisp enough to make walking an exhilarating delight. It was one of the days, not infrequent in the rainy season, when the clouds draw away for a time, while earth and sky, cleansed and refreshed by the recent showers, shine with the refulgence of the rarest mornings of our Western springtime.

As we went out of the old city of Homs, the clearness of the atmosphere was like transparency made visible. The horizon was as clean-cut as that of the ocean. Off to the west were the heights inhabited by the cruel and fanatical Nusairiyeh; straight in front of us to the south was the "Entering In of Hamath," lying low and narrow between Anti-Lebanon on our left and the snow-clad summits of highest Lebanon on our right; while to the east the great wheat-fields of the "Land of Homs" rolled away over the horizon to the unseen desert. Our goal, the little village of Feruzi, shone so white and distinct that it was hard to realize that it was over an hour's journey away.

We were four: two Americans, the native pastor of the Protestant congregation at Homs, and an old, old man. The pastor was a noble fellow, who shortly afterward showed heroic mettle during a fearful cholera epidemic which ravaged his city. The old man, however, was the more picturesque figure.

He was clothed in baggy trousers of faded blue, with a large turban on his head and a heavy, formless sheepskin mantle over his shoulders; his bare feet were thrust into great yellow slippers which flopped clumsily as he walked. We should once have been inclined to treat him with some condescension; but fortunately we had learned the Oriental lesson of reverence for old age, and we American college graduates soon found there were many things that this unschooled Syrian mechanic could teach us. What dignity and quietness marked his speech and manner! How calm and trustful was his attitude toward the future! He was one of the first Protestants in this district, and many were the stories he could tell of the early days of struggle and persecution. He had never been rich — I doubt if he earned thirty cents a day; yet he spoke as one who had observed much and reflected much and, although many kinds of trouble had come to him, his contentment and faith were an inspiration to us. As we were his guests, we were of course treated with the greatest friendliness, yet we could see that in his eyes we were mere boys, who knew little of the problems of life. And, to tell the truth, before the day was over we were more than half inclined to agree with him.

Feruzi is one of the few remaining villages in the country which are not Syrian, but the older Chaldean in blood and language. Its inhabitants, who number about a thousand, appear quite different in feature as well as dress from the people of the surrounding district. Their costume is a peculiar one, remarkable for its warm colors and long, queerly cut trimmings. The women remind one of American Indians, and the faces of the men are of unusual fierceness. It seemed quite natural that there should be a Chaldean church here, big and gaudy, yet ugly and ill-kept, with a much-prized copy of the Scriptures in the Syriac tongue chained to the lectern; but we saw no structure resembling a Protestant place of worship, and among the crowds that followed us curiously about it was impossible to find any one who looked like a Presbyterian elder.

Yet when we turned into the room set apart for the use of the Protestant congregation, some of the wildest and most dangerous-looking men followed. It was a small place, not over twenty feet square, low and dark, and quite bare save for a rough matting on the floor and a chair and a table for the preacher. In a few minutes it was crowded to suffocation. There were over ninety people in the little room. The men sat on one side and the women on the other; but all of us sat on the floor and were so packed together that any change of position was quite impossible, except for a few mothers with babies, who sat near the door.

Throughout the long Christmas sermon the cramped audience showed a reverence and an attentiveness that would have shamed many an American congregation. Suppose that a full-blooded Arab in his flowing native dress, should enter one of our churches at home — what a craning of necks there would be, and how few persons would be able to recall the text! We appeared just as outlandish to the people of Feruzi; yet, although we sat at the back of the room, not a person turned to look at us, except that the man at my side would always help me find the place in the hymn book. It was not indifference, but consideration for the stranger and respect for the occasion; and we who had come merely to see an unusual sight, stayed to worship God with these new friends, and went away with a fuller realization of the meaning of Christmas.

After the service was over, however, there could be no charge of indifference brought against these Chaldean villagers — and here too American congregations might well learn from them. The same men who just now had seemed to ignore our existence came crowding around to greet us as "brethren." They inquired about our life at Beirut and our own wonderful country far beyond the western ocean; they expressed a complimentary surprise at the extent of our travels; they sympathized tenderly with the homesickness which comes so strongly at Christmas-time and expressed kindly wishes for our dear ones in America; they pressed upon us the poor hospitality that it was in their power to offer. In short, out of church as in church, the people of Feruzi acted like the devout, courteous and friendly Christians that they were.

When at last we had to leave, they all followed us out to the village limits, and one or two — such is the pleasant Oriental custom — walked on with us for a mile on our homeward journey. When the last strange, dark Chaldean had said "God be with you, brother!" we went on in the beautiful calm of evening a little more quietly than we had come, with a clearer understanding of the brotherhood of man, and a deeper faith in the teachings of man's great Brother.

To those who look to see an effective Gospel brought again to the Near East through a reawakening of the ancient Oriental churches, it is encouraging to know that even now there are prelates who are earnest, sincere and capable. Such a one was Butrus Jureijery, the first bishop of Cæsarea Philippi and later the patriarch of the Greek Catholic Church.

From beginning to end he was a thoroughgoing Catholic. Indeed, the most striking incident of his early career was an argument with a Protestant Bible-seller, which developed into a fierce fistic combat, with the result that the governor of Lebanon exiled both parties from their native town of Zahleh.

Some years later, after he had been ordained priest, Butrus journeyed to Rome and presented to the Holy Father a novel petition.

"We Catholics," he said, "build our church upon St. Peter, the first bishop, the rock, the holder of the keys; and we remember that the apostle's divine commission was given by Christ at Cæsarea Philippi on the slopes of Mount Hermon. How is it that the original bishopric of the Christian Church, the first see of Peter, has been so long allowed to remain unoccupied?" Now Butrus is the Arabic pronunciation of Peter. So he continued, "Here am I, bearing the very name of the greatest apostle, a native of the holy land of Lebanon, and ready to take up the arduous labors which shall reclaim for the church its first, long neglected bishopric."

The pope was so struck by the force of the argument that he promised to consecrate the young priest as bishop of Cæsarea, or Banias, as it is now called. Then the bishop-elect went through France, preaching a kind of new crusade. His idea was novel and striking, and met with enthusiastic approval. Indeed, with such eloquence did he appeal for the proposed diocese that he became immensely popular throughout all France, and gifts for the Bishopric of

Banias continued to flow in from that country as long as Butrus lived.

In 1897 the highest ecclesiastics of the Greek Catholic Church gathered in solemn convention at Serba to elect a new patriarch. Butrus Jureijery was the people's choice; but the odds against him seemed overwhelming. He was too active and too honest for the hierarchy. The Turkish government was inimical to him, the powerful Jesuit order fought him, the papal nuncio objected to his nomination, and the bishops, almost to a man, opposed him.

For once, however, the Syrian peasants defied their ecclesiastical lords. Word was sent to the convention that its members need not return to their dioceses unless they cast their votes for Butrus. So, in spite of government, Jesuits, papal nuncio, and the wishes of the very electors themselves, the enterprising bishop of Banias became "Patriarch of Antioch, Jerusalem, Alexandria and the Whole East," and, subject to a hardly more than nominal allegiance to the Vatican, the supreme head of a great church whose five million adherents are scattered throughout the Near East from Hungary to Persia and from the Black Sea to the upper Nile.

He had been elected as the "People's Patriarch," and such he remained. A religious and political autocrat, with every opportunity and every precedent for using his office to enrich himself and his family, he remained poor and honest to the end. This means more than the American reader realizes. Throughout the East, political or ecclesiastical office is supposed to afford a quasi-legitimate means of amassing wealth. Few princes of the church have ended their lives in poverty, nor have their families known want. Yet when Butrus died, his own brother would have been unable to attend the funeral, if a popular subscription had not raised sufficient money to buy him a decent coat.

Butrus was progressive as well as honest. His personal beliefs did not change, but, as he grew older, he showed a more liberal spirit toward those who differed with him. He entered into no more fist-fights with his opponents; on the contrary, he treated them with the greatest courtesy. He was the first Greek Catholic patriarch, for instance, to return the calls of the Americans in Beirut or to visit the English Mission at Baalbek. Indeed, at one time four of the seven teachers in his own patriarchal school were Protestants. A thorough churchman himself, he learned to fight dissent with its own weapons; not anathema, excommunication and seclusion, but education, honesty and progress. He presented the spectacle of a man devout of heart and noble of purpose, but differing with some of the rest of us in his theological beliefs. Such are honored by all who hold character above creed.

He was loved by his people and admired and respected by the members of all other communions; but with his own bishops he had to wage unceasing warfare, and the contest drove him into an early grave.

Then they clothed the dead man in his richest robes, heavy with gold and jewels. They put his pontifical staff in his hand and set him on his throne in his palace, and for three days all the world thronged to see him. There were foreign consuls, come to do honor to the wise statesman, Protestant missionaries who esteemed the great Catholic for his honesty and courage, careless young people drawn by news of the strange spectacle, and thousands upon thousands of Butrus' beloved poor, who kissed his cold hand and prayed to him with absolute confidence that he would still be their friend and protector.

On a bright, beautiful Easter Sunday I watched his funeral procession pass through the streets of Beirut. In a way, this last journey was typical of his life and character. For the first time in many long centuries, all sects ignored their differences so that they might together do honor to the prelate who was greater than his church. Roman Catholic, Greek Catholic, Greek Orthodox, Maronite and Armenian marched together; and as the cortège passed the little Protestant Church, its bell was tolled "in order that," as its pastor said, "the Turkish soldiers in the barracks yonder may know that, after all, we Christians are one."

First came three companies of Turkish soldiers and sixty gorgeously dressed consular guards; then chil-

The dead Patriarch being driven through the streets of Beirut in his gilded chariot

A summer camp in Lebanon

dren from the church schools, black-robed Jesuits, humble mourners from the patriarch's native town of Zahleh, men bearing wreaths and banners sent from sister churches; then more children singing a plaintive Arabic hymn. There were present two patriarchs of other communions, more than a dozen bishops and three hundred and fifty priests, and the solemn dignity of the procession, so different from the loud, hysterical wailing at most Syrian funerals, seemed to impress even the Moslem spectators on the housetops along the line of march.

Last of all came Butrus himself, not lying within a black-draped hearse but, as if in triumphal procession, seated in a gilded chariot hung with bright banners and wreaths of flowers. The patriarch sat upright in his gorgeous robes, his staff grasped firmly in one rigid hand and a crucifix in the other. I stood within ten feet of the chariot as it passed by, and there was nothing in the least harrowing in the sight; on the contrary, it was wonderfully dignified and impressive. I could hardly realize that the patriarch was dead; he sat there so naturally with his long gray beard resting upon his golden vestments, and his large, calm features seemed still to be animated by the vital power of his dauntless spirit.

Afterwards there were long addresses lauding the character and good deeds of the dead man; the bishops who had shortened his life said masses for the repose of his soul; and then, still clothed in his robes of state, they placed him on a throne in a vault under the pavement of the cathedral choir. There he sits in solemn, lonely grandeur, like some Eastern Barbarossa waiting for the time when the spirit of the Christ shall be re-born in the church which he so loved, for which in his own earnest way he so unceasingly labored, and for which at last he died.

CHAPTER XII

THE CEDARS OF THE LORD

WE had watered our horses, eaten the last olive and the last scrap of dusty bread that remained in the bottom of our saddle-bags, and were shivering and impatient and irritable; for a sea of beautiful but chilling clouds was rolling around us, and as yet there was no sound of the far-off tinkle that would herald the approach of the belated mule-train which bore our tents and food.

Then suddenly, just as the sun was setting, a friendly breeze swept the clouds down into the valleys; and in a moment fatigue, vexation and hunger were forgotten, as we contemplated one of the most beautiful panoramas in all Lebanon. Before us the mountain sloped quickly to a precipice whose foot lay unseen, thousands of feet below, while just across the gorge, so steep and lofty and apparently so near as almost to be oppressive, towered *Jebel el-Arz* — the Cedar Mountain. The whole range was bathed in a wonderful golden hue, more brilliant yet more ethereal than the alpenglow of Switzerland. Soon the gold faded into blue, and that to a Tyrian purple, a color so royal that those who have not seen cannot believe, so deep and strange that, to those who have seen, it seems almost unearthly. One must gaze and gaze in a vain attempt to fathom its unsearchable depths, until the purple darkens into black, and the watcher stands silent, as if the setting sun had for a moment swung open the door that leads into the eternal.

"Where are the cedars?" I asked a member of our party who had visited them before.

"Over there, directly in front of you!"

"But the mountain seems to be one bare, empty mass of rock!"

"Look closer — yonder — where I am pointing!"

Yes, there they are, apparently hung against the face of the rock in such a precarious situation that a loosened cone would drop clear of the little ledge and fall all the way to the bottom of the valley. You see just a tiny patch of dark green against the mountainside — as big as the palm of your hand — no, as large as a finger nail — like a speck on the lens of a field-glass. Such is the first view of the group of ancient trees which are still known as the "Cedars of the Lord."

While we were engrossed with the mountain scenery, the baggage-train at last appeared. Then came that most satisfyingly luxurious experience, a camp dinner after a long, wearisome day in the saddle. We supplemented our canned food by purchases made at the near-by village of Diman, where we procured delicious grapes, tomatoes, fresh milk, and new-laid eggs at six cents a dozen.

After dinner a young Maronite priest came up from the convent to visit us. Father Abdullah proved to be the private secretary of the patriarch, who has a summer residence at Diman. It was an unanticipated experience for us to meet, high up in this wild mountain region, a Syrian priest who, after graduating from the Maronite College at Beirut, had spent seven years in advanced Latin studies at Paris and had then read archæology at the British Museum. Father Abdullah's English, however, was a broken reed; so most of our conversation was carried on in French, with an occasional lapse into Arabic. He said that his long residence at Paris had naturally brought him into closest sympathy with the French, but that nevertheless he considered the English superior in practicality and energy. He had recently made an independent archæological study of the surrounding district, and entertained us by telling some of his own theories concerning the very early history of Lebanon. Later in the evening, as a further evidence of his friendship, he sent us a great basket of fresh figs.

While we were enjoying this delicious gift, the fog rolled up again from the west and filled the gorge until we looked across the billowing surface of a milk-white sea, above which only a few of the loftiest peaks appeared as lonely islands. Such was the marvelous purity of the air at this altitude that even at night the sky was still a deep blue and the full moon touched the rocks with delicate tints of orange and rose, while, to complete the soft beauty of the scene, a double lunar rainbow swung its cold silvery arcs above the summit of the Cedar Mountain.

Then the wind freshened, the rising fog-waves overflowed from the valleys and the penetrating chill of our cloud-bound mountainside drove us to the shelter of our tents.

When we reached the cedar grove the next noon, we found that our first impressions had been wrong concerning everything except the supreme beauty of the mountain setting. Far from being situated upon a narrow shelf on a perilously steep slope, the trees are securely enthroned amid surroundings of massive grandeur. The watershed of Lebanon here curves around so that it encloses a tremendous natural amphitheater about twelve miles long and over six thousand feet in depth, with its inner, concave side facing the Mediterranean. High up on this crescent-shaped slope, the Kadisha or "Holy" River issues from a deep cave and falls to the bottom of the valley in a succession of beautiful cascades. Around the amphitheater run a succession of curving ledges, like titanic balconies, which near the bottom are small and fertile, but which become longer and broader and more barren toward the wind-swept summits. The highest of these, which lies nearly seven thousand feet above the sea, is eight miles long and at its widest three miles across. Though it is really broken by hundreds of hills, these are dwarfed into insignificance by the great peaks which rise behind them, and in a distant view the surface of the plateau seems perfectly level.

Here, amid surroundings of rare beauty and yet of solemn loneliness, is set the royal throne of the king of trees. Just back of the cedars the mountains rise to an elevation of over 11,000 feet. Around them is vast emptiness and silence. No other trees grow on this chill, wind-swept height. No underbrush springs up among their rugged trunks. The last cultivated fields stop just below, and the nearest village is out of sight and sound, far down the mountainside. A few goatherds lead their flocks to a near-by spring that is fed from the snow-pockets of the Cedar Mountain; but at night the wolves can be heard howling hungrily, and by the end of the year the snow drifts deep around the old trees and the passes are closed for the winter.

Yet downward from the cedars is a prospect of warm, fertile beauty. You look deep into the dark green valley of the Kadisha, and then across the lower mountains to where, thirty miles away, the "great sea in front of Lebanon"[1] rises high up into the sky; and during one memorable week in the summer you can see, a hundred and fifty miles across the

[1] Joshua 9:1.

Mediterranean, the jagged mountain peaks of the island of Cyprus outlined sharp against the red disk of the setting sun.

When the Old Testament writers wished to describe that which was consummately beautiful, rich, strong, proud and enduring, they drew their similes from Hermon and Lebanon, and the climax of the "glory of Lebanon" they found in the "cedars of God."[2] Would they express the full perfection of that which was choice,[3] excellent,[4] goodly,[5] high and lifted up,[6] they pictured "a cedar in Lebanon with fair branches, and with a forest-like shade. . . . Its stature was exalted above all of the trees of the field; and its boughs were multiplied, and its branches became long. . . . All the birds of the heavens made their nests in its boughs; and under its branches did all the beasts of the field bring forth their young. . . . Thus was it fair in its greatness, in the length of its branches . . . nor was any tree in the garden of God like unto it for beauty."[7]

The cedar of Lebanon must not be confounded with the various smaller trees which in America are known as "cedars." It is own brother to the great deodar or god-tree of the Himalayas and the forest giants on the high slopes of the Atlas, Taurus and Amanus ranges. In the days when Hiram of Tyre provided

2 Psalm 80:10.
3 Jeremiah 22:7.
4 Song of Songs 5:15,
5 Ezekiel 17:23.
6 Isaiah 2:13.
7 Ezekiel 31:3f.

timber for Solomon's Temple, large cedar woods spread over Lebanon, and apparently grew also on the sides of Anti-Lebanon and Hermon; but generation after generation these trees became fewer in number. Even in the sixth century, Justinian found it difficult to secure sufficiently large beams for the Church of the Virgin (now the Mosque el-Aksa) in Jerusalem. Many efforts were made to preserve the trees, which had long been considered of a peculiar sanctity. High up on the rocky sides of Lebanon, Hadrian carved his imperial command that the groves should be left untouched. Modern Maronite patriarchs have excommunicated those who cut down the "trees of God." But the roving goats who nibble the tender young saplings have regarded neither emperor nor patriarch. Now there is little timber of any kind in Syria, and the profiles of the mountains cut sharp against the sky. Of the cedars there remain only seven groups, the finest of which is the one we are visiting, above the village of Besherreh.

A former governor of Lebanon, Rustum Pasha, protected this grove against roving animals by a well-built stone wall, and in recent years the number of young trees has consequently slightly increased. But the really old cedars grow fewer century by century; indeed, young and old together, their number is pathetically few. Twelve of the very largest are usually counted as the patriarchs of the grove. The mountaineers say that these had their origin when

Christ and the eleven faithful Disciples once visited Lebanon, and each stuck his staff into the earth, where it took root and became an undying cedar. In all there are about four hundred trees. A local tradition says that they can never be counted twice alike; and, in fact, I have yet to find two travelers who agree as to the number. We need not, however, seek a miraculous explanation of this peculiar lack of unanimity. It is doubtless due to the fact that several trunks will grow so close together that no one can say whether they should be considered as a single tree, or as two or more. When no fewer than seven trunks almost touch at the bottom, it is quite impossible to tell whether they sprang originally from one seed or from many.

Yet though the cedars are few in number, these few are kingly trees. Their height is never more than a hundred feet; but some have trunks over forty feet around, and mighty, wide-spreading limbs which cover a circle two or three hundred feet in circumference. Those which have been unhindered in their growth are tall and symmetrical; others are gnarled and knotted, with room for the Swiss Family Robinson to keep house in their great forks. Some years ago a monk lived in a hollow of one of the trunks. When you climb a little way into a cedar and look out over the whorl of horizontal branches, the upper surface seems as smooth and soft as a rug, upon which have apparently fallen the uplifted cones. Indeed,

The Cedar Mountain. The grove shows as a small, dark patch at the right

The source of the Kadisha River. The rocks in the background mark the edge of the plateau on which are situated the Cedars of Lebanon

the close-growing foliage will bear you almost as well as a carpeted floor. Eighty feet above the ground, I have thrown myself carelessly down, not upon a bough, but upon just the network of interlacing twigs, and rested as securely as if I had been lying in an enormous hammock.

Most of the cedars are crowded so closely that their growth has been very irregular. Sometimes two branches from different trees rub against each other until the bark is broken; then the exuding sap cements them together, and in the course of years they grow into each other so that you cannot tell where one tree ends and the other begins. Just over my tent two such Siamese Twins were joined by a common bough a foot in diameter. Near by I found three trees thus united, and another traveler reports having seen no fewer than four connected by a single horizontal branch which apparently drew its sap from all of the parent and foster-parent trunks. Even more remarkable is a cedar which has been burned completely through near the ground, and yet draws so much sap from an adjoining tree that its upper branches continue to bear considerable foliage.

The wood is slightly aromatic, hard, very close-grained, and takes a high polish. It literally never rots. The most striking characteristic of the cedars is their almost incredible vitality. The oldest of all are gnarled and twisted, but they have the rough strength of muscle-bound giants. Each year new cones rise above the broad, green branches, and the balsamic juice flows fresh from every break in the bark. In the words of the Psalmist, they still bring forth fruit in old age, and are full of sap and green. "There is not, and never has been, a rotten cedar. The wood is incorruptible. The imperishable cedar remains untouched by rot or insect." This is not the extravagant statement of a hurried tourist, but the sober judgment of the late Dr. George E. Post, who was recognized as the world's greatest authority on Syrian botany. The whole side of one of the largest trees has been torn away by lightning, but the barkless trunk is as hard as ever. The single enemy feared by a full-grown cedar is the thunderbolt. "The voice of Jehovah . . . breaketh in pieces the cedars of Lebanon."[8] One or two trees felled by this power have lain prostrate for a generation; but their wood will still turn the edge of a penknife. Here and there, visitors to the grove have stripped off a bit of bark and inscribed their names on the exposed wood. "Martin, 1769," "Girandin, 1791"—the edges of the letters are as hard and clear-cut as if they had been carved last season.

It is no wonder that the ancients chose this imperishable timber for their temples. The cedar roof of the sanctuary of Diana of Ephesus is said to have remained unrotted for four hundred years, while the

[8] Psalm 29:5.

beams of the Temple of Apollo at Utica lasted almost twelve centuries.

Probably the wood is so enduring because it grows so slowly. When you are told that a slender shoot, hardly shoulder-high, is ten or twelve years old, you begin to speculate as to the probable age of the patriarchs of the grove. On a broken branch only thirty inches in diameter I once, with the aid of a magnifying glass, counted 577 rings — 577 years. And some of the cedars are forty feet and over in girth! Certainly these must be a thousand years old, probably two thousand. We are tempted to believe that one or two of the most venerable were saplings when the axemen of Hiram came cutting cedar logs for the Temple at Jerusalem. The most rugged and weather-beaten of them all, called the Guardian — surely this hoary giant of the forest has lived through all the ages since Solomon, and from his lofty throne on Lebanon has calmly looked down over Syria and the Great Sea while Jew and Assyrian, Persian and Egyptian, Greek and Roman, Arab and Crusader and Turk, have labored and fought and sinned and died for the possession of this goodly land!

The trees rise on half a dozen little knolls quite near to the edge of the plateau; and within a few minutes' climb are a number of tall, steeple-like rocks which, through the erosion of the softer stone, have become almost entirely cut off from the main mass of the mountain. One such group, known to American residents of Syria as the "Cathedral Rocks," is reached by following a knife-edge ridge far out over the valley. There is barely room for a narrow foot-path along the top, and a misstep would mean a fall of many hundred feet; but at its western end the ridge broadens out into a group of slender, tower-like cliffs. When you stand on the farthest of these there is a feeling of spaciousness and isolation as if you were indeed upon the loftiest pinnacle of some gigantic cathedral, though no man-built spire towers to such a dizzy height.

A half-hour of hard and, in places, dangerous climbing down from the cedars brings one to where the Kadisha River bursts from a cave in the rock. Like many another cavern in Lebanon, this is of great depth and has never been thoroughly explored. We contented ourselves with penetrating it a few hundred feet; for it was impossible to avoid slipping into the stream now and then, and the water, fresh from the snow-pockets on the summits above, was only twelve degrees above the freezing-point. The entrance is barely ten feet in diameter, but the cave soon divides into several branches, one of which is beautifully adorned with translucent stalactites and, about seventy yards from the mouth, leads up to a large rock-chamber. The river flows out from the mountain with great rapidity and, just below the source, leaps over a precipice in a white waterfall forty feet high, so delicate and lacelike in its beauty that it is known as the "Bridal Veil."

Farther down the valley, the monastery of Kanobin hugs the side of a cliff four hundred feet above the river-bed. This is literally "*the* monastery" (Greek, *koinobion*), and is one of the oldest in the land. It is said to have been founded over sixteen hundred years ago by the Roman emperor Theodosius the Great, and for centuries it has been the nominal seat of the Maronite patriarchs. In 1829, Asad esh-Shidiak, the first Protestant martyr of Lebanon, was walled up in a near-by cave. This unfortunate man was chained to the rock by his Maronite persecutors and about his neck was fastened one end of a long rope which hung out through an opening in the cave by the roadside. Each Catholic who passed by gave the rope a vicious tug, and Shidiak soon died of torture and starvation.

The valley of the Holy River is full of old hermits' caves; but these are now untenanted, and we found no monks even at the great convent. In a parallel valley, however, is a monastery which is still crowded and busy. Deir Keshaya boasts a printing-press, a good library and a staff of a hundred monks. This religious retreat has the most secluded and beautiful situation imaginable. It lies in a very narrow cañon hemmed in by sheer rocks. Yet, though surrounded by nature in its most grand and forbidding aspects, the narrow strip of cultivated land along the river bank is rich with verdure, a veritable Garden of the Lord.

The monastery not only spreads along the face of the cliff, but penetrates far into the mountain. What you see of it from without is hardly more than the façade of a huge, rambling structure whose principal part consists of natural caves and chambers rudely cut in the native rock. Through a little wooden door we were admitted to the largest cavern, where we saw, hanging from staples set securely into its walls, a number of great, cruel chains. People who are possessed of devils are fastened here by the neck and ankles, and during the night an angel comes and drives away the demon. The treatment has never been known to fail; for if the morning finds the sufferer still uncured, that merely shows that he did not have a devil after all, but was just an ordinary lunatic for whom the monastery did not promise relief.

Back of the cedars, there are also many fascinating excursions. The ranges of Syria being geologically "old" mountains which are worn and rounded, you can, by taking a somewhat circuitous route, reach almost any summit on horseback, but it is much more fun to go straight up the steepest slopes on foot. About 2,500 feet above the grove is a line of gently rolling plateaus whose stones have been broken and smoothed by millenniums of snow and ice. You see acre after acre entirely covered with clean, flat fragments which measure from one to five inches in length. Viewed from a distance, their appearance is exactly like that of the soft surface of a wheat-field. The only vegetable life consists of tiny bunches of a low, hardy plant with wooly gray-green leaves. We saw one little butterfly fluttering about lonesomely in the vast desolation.

Sheltered from sun and wind just under the highest ridges are snow-pockets — great, funnel-shaped depressions which during the hottest summer send down their moisture through the mountain mass to the cave-born rivers of western Syria. One who has not been there would never suspect how cold it can be in mid-summer on these higher slopes of Lebanon. The direct rays of the sun are, of course, very hot, and the wise traveler protects his head by a pith helmet. Yet the gloomy gorges are always chilly, the wind is biting, and the nights are positively cold. When tenting among the cedars, I slept regularly under heavy blankets, and once or twice reached down in the middle of the night and pulled over me the rug which lay beside my cot. The first time we climbed the mountain back of our camp, the wind was so cold and penetrating that we could remain only a few minutes on the summit, though we wore the heaviest of sweaters and had handkerchiefs tied over our faces.

At another ascent, however, we were more fortunate, for we found only a slight breeze blowing on the summit. The "Back of the Stick," as the natives call this highest ridge of Lebanon, affords a view over the top of all Syria. Northward stretches the long succession of rounded summits, down to the left of which can be seen the white houses of the seaport of Tripoli. To the south are other lofty peaks, though all are lower than ours. Jebel Sunnin, which seems so mighty when viewed from the harbor of Beirut, now lies far below us. Mount Hermon rises still majestic seventy miles away, yet even the topmost peak of great Hermon is not so high as the spot on which we stand. To the east, across the long, broad valley of the Bika', rises the parallel range of Anti-Lebanon. Westward the magnificent amphitheater which we have come to think of as peculiarly our own opens out to where the Mediterranean, like a sheet of beaten gold, seems to slope far up to the azure sky.

Yet, after a while, we turned from this wonderful panorama to indulge in childish play. With a crowbar brought for the purpose, we dislodged large rocks from the summit and sent them spinning down the eastern side of the mountain. Some of them must have weighed several tons, and they tumbled down the slope with tremendous momentum. The first thousand feet they almost took at a bound; then, reaching a more gentle decline, they would spin along on their edges. Now they would strike some inequality and, leaping a hundred yards, land amid a cloud of scattering stones; now they would burst in mid-air from centrifugal force, with a noise like a cannon shot; now some very large stone, surviving the perils of the descent, would arrive at the base of our peak and, on the apparently level plateau below, would very slowly roll and roll and roll as if it possessed some motive power of its own. Several days later we met a wandering shepherd who told us that, while dozing beneath the shade of a cliff far down the mountainside, he had been suddenly awakened by a terrific cannonading and had sat there for hours in trembling wonderment at the demoniac forces which were tumbling Mount Lebanon down over his head.

One evening we strolled out to the edge of our plateau and saw the whole countryside a-twinkle with lights. It was the anniversary of the Finding of the True Cross. When St. Helena, mother of Constantine the Great, discovered the precious relic sixteen hundred years ago, beacons prepared in anticipation of the success of the search were lighted and the glad news was thus flashed from Jerusalem to the emperor at Constantinople. In commemoration of that joyous event, annual signal fires still burn along the land of Lebanon. Far down in black gorges we saw the lights flash out. North and south of us, unseen villages on the hillsides kindled their beacons. Higher up, in wild pine forests, the lonely charcoal-burners made their camp-fires blaze brighter; and even on the bare, bleak summits there shone here and there tiny gleams of light. Amid the solemn quiet of our mountain solitude, we watched the beacons flash out around us and below us and above, until all Lebanon seemed starred with the bright memorials of the Cross which this old, old land, through long centuries of oppression and ignorance and bigotry, has never quite forgot.

We spent a month in the cedar grove, and never had a dull day. At dawn we could look out of the tent to where the green branches framed a charming bit of blue, distant sea. After breakfast the studious man would climb up into his favorite fork and ensconce himself there with pen and ink and paper and books and cushions. The adventurous man would scramble up to the topmost bough of some lofty tree and stretch out on its soft twigs for a sun-bath. The lazy man would curl up against a comfortable root, to smoke and dream away the morning hours. Sketching and photographing and mountain climbs were interspersed with unsuccessful hunting expeditions and aimless conversations with Maronite priests who had come up to visit their little rustic chapel in the grove. After supper came the camp-fire, with its cozy sparkle and its friendly confidences and the black background of the forest all around. Then, by eight o'clock at the latest, we snuggled into our blankets and, in the crisp, balsam-scented air, slept the clock around. Sometimes the full moon shone so brightly that the whole mountain would take on a soft silver glow, against which colors could be distinguished almost as well as by day. Now and then there would be a cold, foggy morning; but the trees kept out the mists and, although a solid wall of white surrounded us, within the grove it was clear and dry and homelike.

The shelter, the support, the background, the inspiration of all the camp life, were the great, solemn trees. After a while you come to love them, or rather to reverence them. They are so large, so old; they have such marked individuality. The cedars are regal rather than beautiful. Rough and knotted and few in number, at first sight they are a little disappointing; but, like the mountains around them, they become more impressive day by day. These thousand-year-old trees seem to stand aloof from the hurry and bustle of the twentieth century, as though they were absorbed in thoughts of earlier, and perhaps wiser, days. After you have lived for a time beneath their shade, their solemn magnificence begins to quiet your spirit; and when the glorious moonlight floods the mountain and casts black shadows down the deep gorges that drop away to the distant sea, it is easy to behold in the witching light the picture that these ancient trees saw in the long ago. Dark groves of cedars nestle once more in the valleys and sweep over the mountain-tops in great waves of green; a stronger peasantry speaks a different tongue in the fields below that are brighter and the orchards that are heavier with fruit; and from the depths of the moon-painted forest there comes the ring of ten thousand axes that are hewing down the choicest trunks for the Temple of the Lord.

Then the vision fades, and with a sense of personal loss and a regret that is almost anger, you look out again from under the dark branches of the little grove to the bleak, bare mountainside, and the wind in the topmost boughs seems to sing the lament of Zechariah —

"Wail, O fir tree,
For the cedar is fallen,
Because the glorious ones are destroyed:
Wail, O ye oaks of Bashan,
For the strong forest is come down."[9]

Yet still some glorious ones of the strong forest rise proudly on their throne in Lebanon. This tree, so beautiful that it is pictured on the seal of the college at Beirut, has been called the Symmetrical Cedar. These many trunks, apparently springing from a single root, we know as the Seven Sisters. Those two that stand side by side without the wall at a little distance from the main group, are the Sentinels. On a hillside are St. John and St. James, immense, fatherly trees with trunks forty-five feet in circumference and gigantic forks in which a dozen people

[9] Zechariah 11:2f.

The Guardian, the oldest Cedar of Lebanon

The six great columns and the Temple of Bacchus

could sit together. Then there is the Guardian, oldest and largest of all, its great trunk twisted and gnarled by struggles against the storms of ages, the names which famous travelers carved a century ago not yet covered by its slowly growing bark. But the knotted, wrinkled, lightning-scarred giant is crowned by a garland of evergreen, and the venerable tree, which perhaps heard the sound of Hiram's axemen, may still be standing proudly erect when the achievements of our own century are dimmed in the ancient past.

"The Cedars of the Lord"—we understand now why the peasantry of Lebanon call them thus. It has become our own name for them too. Long before we ride downward from their royal solitude to the Great Sea and the great busy world, we have come to think of them as in deed and truth,

"The trees of Jehovah . . .
The cedars of Lebanon, which He hath planted."

CHAPTER XIII

THE GIANT STONES OF BAALBEK

THE most impressive of all the ancient temples of Syria can now be reached by a comfortable railway journey from either Damascus or Beirut. But this way the traveler comes upon the ruins too quickly to appreciate adequately their splendid situation and marvelous size. I shall always be thankful that, on my first visit to Baalbek, I approached it very slowly as I rode from our camp among the cedars of Lebanon. For the longer you look at these temples and the greater the distance from which you behold them, the more fully do you realize that whatever race first built a shrine here chose the spot which, of all their land, had the largest, noblest setting for a sanctuary; and the better also do you understand that these structures had to be made unique in their grandeur because anything less imposing would have seemed paltry in comparison with the surrounding glories of nature.

Where the Bika‘ is highest and widest and most fertile, on a foothill of Anti-Lebanon which projects far enough to give a commanding outlook in all directions, stands Baalbek, the City of the Sun-God. Far northward Hollow Syria leads to the open wheat-lands of Homs and Hama; at the south it sinks gently to the foot of Hermon. Back of the city are the peaks of the Eastern Mountains, and across the level valley rise the highest summits of Lebanon. It is no wonder that the approaching traveler finds it difficult at first to realize the magnitude of the ruins. Any work of man would be dwarfed by the magnificent heights which look down upon Baalbek. But what an inspiration these same mountains must have been to the unknown architect who conceived the daring grandeur of the Temple of the Sun!

When I viewed the ruins from the summit of the highest mountain of Lebanon, their columns did not seem especially large. Then I remembered that there are few structures whose details can be distinguished at all from a point twenty miles away. After descending many thousand feet through rocky ravines and dry water-courses, we came out on the Bika‘ and again saw the temples. They now appeared of moderate size and very near. It was hard to believe that a few minutes' canter would not bring us to them and, as we rode across the monotonous level of the valley, it seemed as if each new mile would surely be the last. When I had traveled for an hour straight toward their slender columns and found them apparently as far away as ever, I began to understand that these temples must be of a bigness beyond anything that I had ever seen before.

While we were looking toward Mount Hermon, whose conical summit rose from behind the southern horizon, the hot, shimmering air began to arrange itself in horizontal layers of varying density, and before our wondering eyes there grew a picture of cool and shady comfort. Four or five miles away a grove of date-palms stood beside a beautiful blue lake in which were a number of little islands, each with its cluster of bushes or its group of trees; and, just beyond the islands, the rippling water laved the steep sides of Mount Hermon. It was a cheering sight for the tired traveler. This was no freak of an imagination crazed by privation and exhaustion. Everything was as clear-cut and distinct as were the temples of Baalbek. We knew very well that there was no lake in the Bika' and that Mount Hermon was not within fifty miles of where it seemed to be; yet we agreed upon every detail of the wonderful mirage. We counted the wooded islets; we pointed out to each other the beauty of the shrubbery and the symmetry of the waving palm trees; we remarked upon the sharp reflections of the branches in the clear water. Then, while we looked, the islands began to swim around, the bushes shrank together, the trees shifted their positions, the blue water faded into a misty white, old Hermon receded far into the background — and soon all that was left were two or three dusty palms bowing listlessly over the dry, brown earth in the sizzling heat.

I had always thought of Baalbek as a magnificent ruin in the midst of a wilderness; at best, I expected to find huddled beneath the temples a tiny hamlet like that at Palmyra. But as we came nearer to the spot of green about the columns, it grew larger and larger, and finally opened out into a prosperous-looking town of five thousand inhabitants besides, as we discovered later, a garrison of Turkish soldiers and a host of summer visitors. The bazaars were busy and noisy, and the half-dozen hotels were filled with the cream of Syrian society. Gay young prodigals from Beirut clattered recklessly along on blooded mares, or lolled back in rickety barouches, talking French to pretty girls whose silk dresses were so nearly correct that our masculine eyes could not detect just what was the matter with them.

The German archæologists who were then excavating among the ruins told us that the hotel where we had planned to lodge was incorrectly constructed and would surely fall down some day, and advised us to take rooms at the more substantial building where they were dwelling. Here we found one of those typically cosmopolitan companies which add so much variety to life in Syria. Besides the Germans, there was a suave little Turkish gentleman, a very amiable Armenian lady, a radiantly beautiful Hungarian, an English "baroness" who did not explain where she had obtained this obsolete title, and a couple of those innocently daring American maiden-ladies who blunder unprotected through foreign countries whose languages they do not understand, and yet somehow never seem to get into serious trouble.

Everybody but the American ladies spoke French, so we had several delightful evenings together. With the Armenian we discussed the recent massacres — when the Turkish gentleman was not by. The Hungarian lady discoursed heatedly upon the thesis that the Magyars are not subjects but allies of the Austrian Empire. The baroness told us thrilling tales of social and political intrigues on three continents, some of which we believed. The Germans interpreted enormous drawings of their excavations, and my traveling companion and I sang negro songs to the accompaniment of a tiny, wheezy melodion.

Baalbek is deservedly popular as a summer resort; for its elevation is nearly four thousand feet and, even in August, there are few uncomfortably warm days. In fact, the city has long borne the reputation of being the coolest in Syria. The Arab geographer Mukadassi, who lived in the tenth century, wrote that "among the sayings of the people it is related how, when men asked of the cold, 'Where shall we find thee?' it was answered, 'In the Belka,'[1] and when they further said, 'But if we meet thee not

[1] East of the Jordan, between Jabbok and Arnon rivers.

there?' then the cold answered, 'Verily, in Baalbek is my home.'"

The most attractive features of the city, next to its refreshing climate, are its unusual number of shaded streets and its copious supply of pure, cold water. Both of these are somewhat rare in Syria. In this land of generous orchards, there are very few shade-trees; and during the long, rainless summer the flow of the springs is usually husbanded with great care. In Baalbek, however, the water is allowed to run everywhere in almost reckless abundance. It gushes out of a score of fountains; it drives the mills, waters the gardens and rushes alongside the streets in swift, clear streams. Our own supply for drinking was drawn from one of the springs; but we were told that even the water in the deep roadside gutters was clean and healthful.

On account of the natural advantages of its situation, it is probable that Baalbek has been in existence ever since the time when men first began to build cities. The sub-structures of the acropolis are literally prehistoric, that is, they antedate anything that we know at all certainly about the history of the place. In the Book of Joshua [2] we find three references to "Baal-gad in the valley (Hebrew, *Bika'*) of Lebanon," but the identification of this place with Baalbek is far from certain. The Arab

[2] Joshua 11:17, 12:7, 13:5.

geographers of the twelfth century, who were tremendously impressed by the grandeur of the ruins and the fertility of the surrounding district, believed that the larger temple was built by Solomon, who also had a magnificent palace here, and that the city was given by him as a dowry to Balkis, Queen of Sheba. Benjamin of Tudela, a Spanish rabbi who visited Syria in the year 1163, wrote that when Solomon was laying the heaviest stones, he invoked the assistance of the genii.

It may possibly be that the foundations are even older than the time of Solomon; but there is no historical notice of the city which goes back of the Roman period. Coins of the first century A. D. indicate that it was then a colony of the Empire and was known as Heliopolis, the Greek translation of the Semitic name Baalbek.

During the early centuries of our era Heliopolis became exceedingly prosperous and, indeed, famous. The emperor Antoninus Pius is said to have erected here a temple to Jupiter which was one of the wonders of the world, and coins struck in Syria about 200 A. D., in the reign of Septimius Severus, bear the representations of two temples. During this period the worship of Baal became popular far beyond the borders of Syria, and the Semitic sun-god was identified with the Roman Jupiter. The empress of Severus was daughter of a priest of Baal at Homs, only sixty miles north of Baalbek. When her nephew Varius [3] usurped the throne, he assumed the new imperial title of "High Priest of the Sun-God" and erected a temple to that deity on the Palatine Hill. At Baalbek itself the worship was accompanied by licentious orgies until the conversion of Constantine the Great, who abolished these iniquitous practices, erected a church in the Great Court of the Temple of the Sun, and consecrated a bishop to rule over the still heathen inhabitants of the new see.

Since then, the history of Baalbek has been parallel to that of every other stronghold in Syria, a history of battles and sieges and massacres and a long succession of conquerors with little in common except their cruelty. When the Arabs captured the city in the seventh century, they converted the whole temple area into a fortress whose strategic position, overlooking the Bika' and close to the great caravan routes, enabled it to play an important part in the wars of the Middle Ages. Many a great army has battered at this citadel. Iconoclastic Moslems have done all they could to deface its carvings and statues, earthquake after earthquake has shaken the temples, scores of buildings in the present town have been constructed from materials taken from the acropolis, col-

[3] Varius Avitus Bassanius, who took the name Heliogabalus upon his appointment as high priest of the sun-god, was born at Homs, A. D. 204, usurped the imperial throne at the death of his cousin Caracalla in 218 and, after a brief reign marked chiefly by its infamous debaucheries, was murdered by the Prætorians in 222.

umns and cornices have been robbed of the iron clasps that held their stones together, and for many years the Great Court was choked with the slowly accumulating débris of a squalid village which lay within its protecting walls.

Yet neither iconoclast nor sapper, artilleryman nor peasant, has been able to destroy the majesty of the temples of Baalbek. The malice of the image-breaker cannot tumble down thousand-ton building-blocks and grows weary in the effort to deface cornices eighty feet above him. Mosques and khans, barracks and castle walls have been built out of this immense quarry of ready-cut stone, yet the supply seems hardly diminished. The cannonballs of the Middle Ages fell back harmless before twenty feet of solid masonry, and only God's earthquake has been able to shake the massive foundations of the Temple of Baal.

The old walls of the acropolis provide many a tempting place for an adventurous clamber. Beside the main gateway at the eastern end you can ascend a winding stairway, half-choked with rubbish; then comes some hard climbing over broken portions of the upper fortifications and a bit of careful stepping around a narrow ledge on the outside of a turret. But it is well worth a little exertion and risk to reach the top of this majestic portal, where you can lie lazily among great piles of broken carvings and watch the long shadows of the setting sun creep over what have been called "the most beautiful mass of ruins that man has ever seen and the like of which he will never behold again."

Our superlative expressions are prostituted to such base uses that it is hard to find words to picture adequately these colossal structures. To say that they are most majestic, gigantic, stupendous, is only to trifle with terms. The mere partition-wall beneath us is nineteen feet thick, a single stone in one of the gate-towers is twenty-five feet long, and the entrance stairway, now half-buried beneath an orchard, is a hundred and fifty feet wide. Everything about us is immense; yet the parts are so nicely proportioned that at first their size does not seem very unusual. The German archæologists warned me against jumping carelessly from one stone to another. "The distance between them will be greater than you think." You have to revise your ordinary judgments of perspective before you can realize that yonder little alcove in the Great Court is as big as an ordinary church, or can make yourself believe that the outlines of the Temple of the Sun enclose an area as large as that of Westminster Abbey, or can break the habit of thinking condescendingly of the "Smaller Temple"— which is one of the finest Græco-Roman edifices in existence. Suddenly you see the acropolis in its real immensity and beauty, and then you under-

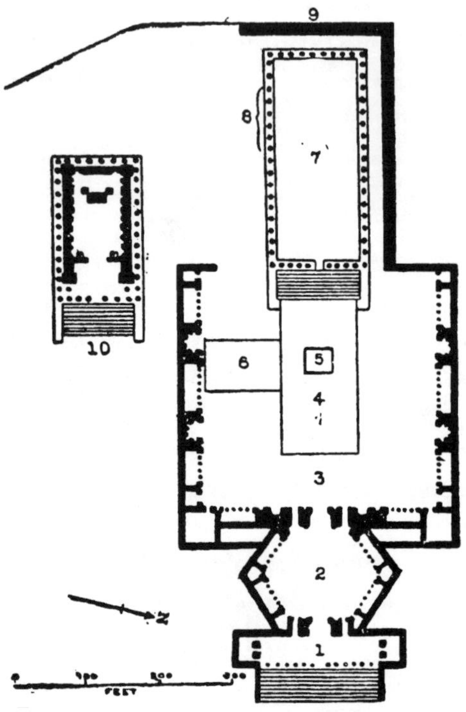

The Acropolis of Baalbek—1, The Propylæa; 2, The Fore-court; 3, The Court of the Altar; 4, The Basilica of Constantine; 5, The Great Altar of the Temple; 6, Byzantine Baths; 7, The Temple of Jupiter-Baal; 8, The Six Standing Columns; 9, The Great Stones in the Foundation Wall; 10, The Temple of Bacchus.

stand how the most scholarly of all Syrian travelers could say that the temples of Baalbek " are like those of Athens in lightness, but far surpass them in vastness; they are vast and massive like those of Thebes, but far excel them in airiness and grace."[4]

From the entrance stairway at the east to the Great Temple at the west, the arrangement is grandly cumulative. Each succeeding architectural feature is larger and more beautiful than that which precedes it. As you view the acropolis from above the portico, your eye is drawn on and on, past the symmetrical forecourt and the great Court of the Altar, under delicately chiseled arches and graceful cornices, through the Triple Gate and the temple portal, up to the culmination of it all — the six tall columns which still rise above the ruins of the Temple of the Sun. No! this is not yet the climax of the glories of Baalbek; for beyond those slender shafts the hoary head of Lebanon, towering far into the sky, at once dwarfs and dignifies, enslaves and ennobles, the puny massiveness of the sanctuary of Baal.

The Great Court, or "Court of the Altar," is littered with sculptured stones — pedestals of statues, inscriptions in Greek and Latin, broken columns, curbs of old wells and fragments of fallen cornices. On each side of the few remains of the Basilica of Constantine are Roman baths, which are carved in a graceful, profuse manner, very like those at Nîmes in southern France.

The sculptors seem to have worked in three shifts. The first were mere stone-cutters who removed sur-

[4] Edw. Robinson, *Biblical Researches in Palestine,* III. 517.

plus material, shaping a hemisphere where a head was to appear in bas-relief, and indicating the rough outlines of leaves and flowers. The second set of workmen carved the design more carefully, leaving it for the third, the master-artists, to give the final touches. In the temple baths we can see traces of the work of all three classes. One part of the carving is finished to the last crinkle of a rose leaf; another is but roughly blocked out by a mere artisan. It seems that the full plan for the courts was never carried to completion. Some think, indeed, that the only portion of the Great Temple itself which was finished was the peristyle.

A little to the southwest of the Court of the Altar stands the Temple of Bacchus. This suffers the fate of great men whose fame is eclipsed by that of their greater brothers. Yet this "Smaller Temple," as it is commonly called, is larger than the Parthenon, and is surpassed in the beauty of its architecture by no other similar edifice outside of Athens. It was originally surrounded by forty-two columns, each fifty-two and a half feet in height. A number of these have been overthrown by earthquakes and cannon-balls, but on the north side the peristyle is still nearly perfect. One of the columns on the south side has fallen against the temple, yet, although made up of three drums, the parts are held so firmly together by iron clamps that it has broken several stones of the wall without itself coming to pieces.

Intricate stone-cut tracery runs riot over the double frieze, the fluted half-columns and niches, and the variously shaped panels which form the roof of the peristyle. There are flowers and fruits and leaves, vines and grapes and garlands, men and women, gods and goddesses, satyrs and nymphs, and the youthful god himself, surrounded by laughing bacchantes. Most elaborate of all is the carving around the lofty central portal, which is probably more exquisite in detail than anything else of its kind in existence. The door-posts are forty feet high, yet they are chiseled with such a delicacy that they seem almost as light as a filigree of Damascus silver-work. Upon the under side of the lintel a great eagle holds a staff in its claws, while from its beak droop long garlands of flowers, the ends of which are held by genii.

Of the Temple of Jupiter-Baal, which was the principal structure of the acropolis, only six columns are now standing; but these six can be seen far up and down the Bika'. As you stand beside them and look up, the columns appear of tremendous bulk, as indeed they are; yet their proportions are so elegant that at a little distance they seem almost frail. When you view them from many miles away, they appear as tenuous as the strings of a colossal harp, awaiting the touch of Æolus himself to set them vibrating in tremendous harmony. Now the columns, crossed by the cornice above, resemble a titanic gate ready to swing open to the Garden of the Gods; now they are seen in profile, like a giant finger pointing upward. When the evening glow falls upon them, the stone takes on a yellowish tinge and the slender shafts look like a golden grating which some old master has put between the panels of his daring picture of brazen clouds and dazzling mountaintops. Even the long colonnades of Palmyra lack something of the peculiar grandeur of the six columns of Baalbek, as they stand guard over the ruined Temple of Baal, with nothing to rival their towering grandeur save the eternal peaks of Lebanon.

Yet, though these columns are the most beautiful things in Baalbek, they are not its greatest marvel; for in the foundations of the acropolis are stones so immense that we can only guess at the means employed to quarry and transport and lift into place these huge masses of rock.

Parallel to the north side of the Temple of the Sun is an outer wall ten feet thick and composed of nine stones, each thirty feet long and thirteen feet high; in the west foundation-wall of the acropolis are seven other stones of equal size, not lying upon the ground but set on lower tiers; and just above these is a series of three stones which are probably the largest ever handled by man.

These tremendous three were so renowned in ancient times that the temple above them came to be known as the *Trilithon.* They are each thirteen feet

The stone in the quarry of Baalbek

The Orontes River at Hama

high, probably ten feet thick, and their lengths are respectively sixty-three, sixty-three and a half, and sixty-four feet. It is hard to realize their true dimensions, however; for these enormous blocks are set into the wall twenty-three feet above the ground, and are fitted together so closely that you can hardly insert the edge of a penknife between them. Look at them as long as you will, you can never fully see their bigness. Yet if only one were taken out of the wall, a space would be left large enough to contain a Pullman sleeping-car. Each stone, though it seems only of fitting size for this noble acropolis, weighs as much as many a coastwise steamer. If it were cut up into building blocks a foot thick, it would provide enough material to face a row of apartment houses two hundred feet long and six stories high. If it were sawn into flag-stones an inch thick, it would make a pavement three feet wide and over six miles in length.

The quarry from which was taken the material for the temples is about three-quarters of a mile from the acropolis. Here lies a still larger stone which, on account of some imperfection, was never completely separated from the mother rock. By this time we have no breath left for exclamations; hyperbole would be impossible; the simple measurements are astounding enough. The *Hajr el-Hibla*,[5] as it is called, is thirteen feet wide, fourteen feet high, seventy-one

[5] Literally, "the stone of the pregnant woman." Bearing in mind the meaning of the popular name, the reader will easily

feet long, and would weigh at least a thousand tons. It does not arouse our wonderment, however, as much as do those other stones, only a little smaller, which were actually finished and built into the wall.

How, indeed, were such huge blocks moved from the quarry to the acropolis? How were they lifted into place and fitted so nicely together? The question has not been answered to our entire satisfaction. We must acknowledge that those old Syrians — if they *were* Syrians — could perform feats of engineering that would challenge the science of the present day. The most plausible guess is that a long incline was built all the way from the quarry to the temple wall and then, through a prodigal expenditure of time and labor, the blocks were moved slowly up the regular slope, a fraction of an inch at a time, by balancing them back and forth on wooden rollers. But it is almost as easy to believe with the natives that there were giants in those days, and that the great stone which is still in the quarry was being carried along under her arm by a young woman, when she heard her baby cry, and so dropped her burden and left it there to be the wonderment of us puny folk.

understand just how and why I have modified the frank, Oriental form of the story which follows.

CHAPTER XIV

HAMATH THE GREAT

NOW that the French railway system has at last extended its operations into northern Syria, the old cities of Homs and Hama will doubtless soon lose much of their naïveté and Oriental color and become filled with dragomans who speak a dozen languages and shopkeepers who have a dozen prices for the unwary tourist. Up to the present, however, the district has been little touched by Western civilization, and we saw there a picture of Syrian life and customs, and especially of unspoiled Syrian politeness, not to be found in more accessible cities.

We traveled from the seaport of Tripoli to Homs in a big yellow diligence, drawn by two horses and three mules, and driven by a couple of unkempt brigands who, in the absence of a sufficiently long whip, urged on their steeds by throwing heavy stones taken from a well-filled bushel-basket which was kept under the seat. The Syrians ordinarily throw like girls, and with as good an aim; but these men, while the coach was rolling and creaking like a ship in a storm, could strike the left ear of the farthest mule without any danger either to its own skull or to the other animals.

This ugly, noisy conveyance, which took us sixty miles in eleven hours, seemed quite out of place as a part of the Syrian landscape, and we noticed that it surprised the rest of the country as much as it had us. The camels were the most astonished. Along the road would be seen approaching a distant caravan, led by a white-bearded old man riding a ridiculously small donkey. Behind him, the long line of great animals walked and chewed in a slow rhythm, and looked out upon the world with a solemn gaze which made us flippant sons of a young republic feel like crawling away somewhere and hiding for a few thousand years until we had acquired a little mellowness.

But our mules represented the spirit of modern progress; on a down grade, it was progress at the dizzying speed of ten miles an hour. Now, viewed from the front, a camel looks like an overgrown chicken, and when he is startled he acts just like a flustered fowl. So we had the interesting experience of frightening half to death thirty of these great, clumsy creatures, who scampered and scattered over the road in every direction except the right one, ran into one another and knocked off carefully balanced loads, and tied up the connecting ropes into intricate knots which would challenge the genius of an Alexander to untangle, while a dozen or so stalwart

Arabs cursed us with a choice of vituperation not to be found in our more stolid West — cursed with a long, deep, comprehensive curse which included us and our fathers, the diligence's father and mother and distant relatives, and laid special emphasis upon the awful destruction which was sure to overtake the religion of the off mule.

About an hour's journey from Tripoli there is a very old pool of sacred fish, references to which are found in works of travel as early as the sixth century. According to the present tradition, the souls of soldiers who have died fighting for Islam are reincarnated in these fish. The Moslems accordingly hold them in the greatest reverence; and if anyone, particularly if a Christian, should harm them, he would almost certainly be torn to pieces by an infuriated mob. While thousands of men and women in the neighboring villages may be suffering the pangs of hunger, wealthy zealots will buy great piles of bread for the fish; often, indeed, they provide in their wills for a certain number of loaves to be thrown each week into the pool. The fish, which are about a foot in length, are fat and bloated as a consequence of this over-feeding, and are unspeakably ugly in form and color. We estimated that there were between four and five thousand of them in the little pool; and it was a sight not soon to be forgotten, as they crowded after the crumbs which we threw them, pushing and fighting so that they were often forced quite out of their element and for many square yards the water was completely hidden by the loathsome, wriggling mass.

After eight hours' drive along the valley that leads from Tripoli into the interior, a sudden turn of the road brought into full view the great plain of north-eastern Syria. We were entering this through a break in its western wall, the pass which divides Lebanon from the Nusairiyeh Range, inhabited by its cruel, half-pagan tribes. At our right, the southern margin of the plain was distinctly marked by the abrupt ending of Anti-Lebanon and of the nearer Bika'. The place where the central valley of Syria opens suddenly to the broad expanse of wheat country was known of old as the "Entering In of Hamath," and was the northernmost point to which the Kingdom of Israel ever extended.[1] At the left, low hills rise slowly up to the horizon; in front, the plain rolls out to the unseen desert and the ruined palaces of Palmyra.

[1] Many eminent scholars, however, follow Edward Robinson (*Biblical Researches*, III. 568) in identifying the "Entering In of Hamath" (Judges 3:3, I Kings 8:65, etc.), not with the northern end of the Bika', but with the east-and-west valley between the Lebanon and Nusairiyeh ranges, through which we have just come. While I incline more and more toward the view given in the text above, the question must be decided by one's feeling as to which would be the more striking and appropriate landmark, rather than by any direct evidence. The territory included would be practically the same in either case.

It is one of the world's greatest battlefields that lies below us, so vast that Waterloo and Gettysburg might be fought in different corners and hardly see the smoke of each other's cannonading. But no modern conflict has engaged such hosts as were drawn up here in martial array. They came from the desert capital, came up from Palestine and Egypt by way of the Entering In of Hamath, came as we have come, through the narrow pass leading from the Mediterranean. Back at the beginning of wars, the trained armies of Egypt fought the Hittite and the Chaldean here. After Babylonian and Persian, Jew and Syrian and Greek had become mere subjects of imperial Rome, it was here that Zenobia, the beautiful, talented, ambitious queen of Palmyra, received her crushing defeat at the hands of Aurelian. Here, centuries later, Crusader and Saracen battled for the land they both called Holy; here chivalrous Tancred led his armies and valiant Saladin won decisive victories.

Two things stand out from the general brownness of the plain. Just below us is the dazzling white acropolis of Homs, and ten miles to the south is the deep blue of the lake once called *Qadesh*, the "Holy," which was dammed up in its little valley by a long-vanished race and worshiped before history began.

We saw the bright reflection from the smooth sides of the mound long before we could distinguish the town lying beneath it, and for a while we were puzzled as to what it was — this huge, symmetrical object rising so abruptly from the great, flat plain, and seeming doubly immense because of the clear air and the absence of any neighboring elevation with which to compare its height. The acropolis is, indeed, no insignificant structure. The people of Homs believe it to be entirely artificial, and its appearance is in favor of such an hypothesis. The circular hill is almost a thousand feet in diameter and its platform stands a hundred feet above the plain. The sides rise so steeply that it would be impossible to scale them without a ladder; and, to make the summit absolutely inaccessible to an enemy, all the outer slope of the mound formerly bore a slippery coating of small, square basalt blocks. At present the platform is reached by a long, winding path; but even this is so steep as to be almost dangerous in places. During the Crusades the fortress of Homs was held alternately by the Christians and the Saracens; and it has suffered from so many assaults that nothing of the old castle now remains save a few fragments of tumbling wall and a ruined gateway.

As we came down into the plain and had a nearer view of the acropolis, we seemed to distinguish a multitude of houses beneath it; but the difficulty of getting a true perspective had deceived us. The city lay beyond and lower; what we now saw were not houses but graves. It was a great metropolis of the dead; thousands and tens of thousands of mounds were crowded close together at the foot of the fortress-hill. Some few were surmounted by stone canopies; but most of them were simple Moslem graves, ranged in long ranks looking toward the sacred city of Mecca, with one stone at the head and another at the foot, for the two angels to rest upon as they weigh the good and evil deeds of the dead. As one approaches nearly every great Syrian city, this is the order of interest and impressiveness; first the ruins of former power and grandeur, then the graves of those who trusted in that power and gloried in that grandeur, last the modern town with its poverty and squalor and ignorance.

In Greek times "Emesa," as it was then called, was a place of no little size and importance, and during the Roman era one of its sons wore the imperial purple [2] and one of its daughters became empress.[3] The modern city contains some sixty thousand inhabitants, the large majority of whom are Moslems. The Christians are nearly all Orthodox "Greeks," but there is also a tiny Protestant community. We were guests of the native pastor, and later it lent a new impressiveness to our memories of Homs when we learned that our host was stabbed the very week after our visit. Fortunately, however, the wound was not a mortal one. The city is the market-place of *Ard Homs*, "the Land of Homs," and its bazaars are

[2] Heliogabalus. See foot-note, page 191.
[3] Julia Domna, wife of Septimius Severus.

crowded with *fellahîn* from all the country round about. The chief industry is the weaving of silks. The citizens claim that there are five thousand looms, and it is easy to believe this statement; as we walked along the streets, which were well-paved and cleaner than those of most Syrian towns, there were whole blocks where every house resounded with the whirring of wheels and the clicking of shuttles.

The home of our host, like almost every other residence in Homs, opened on a court which was separated from the street by a ten-foot wall. We rose at three o'clock the next morning to catch the diligence for Hama, said good-by all around in the lengthy Arabic fashion — and discovered that the key to the one gate was lost. Thereupon arose great bustle and confusion; the women rushed around looking everywhere for the missing key, while the worthy pastor brought a clumsy ladder to help us over the wall. But just as we were preparing to carry our heavy luggage up the ladder, the key was found, and a hard run brought us to the diligence with half a minute to spare.

This second coach had only two mules and one horse, and was a much smaller affair than that which had brought us from Tripoli. Although the driver was a Moslem to whom alcoholic beverages are strictly forbidden, he was considerably more than half-drunk. He had neglected to fasten the harness properly and, while we were rattling down a steep hill, the tangle of straps and strings dropped off one beast and dangled under his heels. Then, as soon as the harness was repaired, our driver let his reins fall among the flying hoofs. He took these mishaps very philosophically; much more so, to tell the truth, than we did. Doubtless he pitied us Western infidels for our evident nervousness and lack of faith. Suppose that the coach should indeed upset — it would be the will of Allah, and who were we to object!

We had but one fellow-traveler, a fat old Moslem wearing the turban of a *haj* who has made the pilgrimage to Mecca. He was a most companionable fellow who insisted upon explaining to us all the points of interest along the road; and the fact that his explanations were usually wrong did not in the least detract from our enjoyment of his company. Every time the diligence stopped — and, with our drunken driver and worn-out harness, this was quite often — the Haj would laboriously descend, spread out his handkerchief upon some clean, level spot alongside the road, and turn toward Mecca to recite his prayers. He must have been a very holy man.

The road from Homs to Hama runs almost due north, a straight white line cutting across the green fields. It is one of the oldest highways in the world. For at least five thousand years caravans have been passing along it just as we saw them — long strings of slow-moving camels laden with brightly colored bags of wheat. One could almost imagine that

Pharaoh was again calling down the corn of Hamath to fill his granaries against the impending seven years of famine. But even here the old things are passing. Just beyond the line of camels, a longer line of peasant women, with dirty blue dresses kilted above their knees, were carrying upon their heads baskets of earth and stone for the road-bed of the new French railway. The carriage road is French, too; and a very good road it is. We noticed some men repairing it with a most ingenious roller. A huge rounded stone, drawn by two oxen, had its axle prolonged by a twenty-foot pole, at the end of which a bare-legged Syrian was fastened to balance the contrivance. If the stone had chanced to topple over, the spectacle of the captive road-maker dangling at the top of the slender flag-staff would have been well worth watching.

All along the journey we were reminded of the fact that this was not only the East, but the old, old East. The soil is fertile, but the very wheat-fields are different from ours. Only a few yards in width, they are often of prodigious length; the thin green strips sometimes stretch away until in the far distance they are lost over the curve of the treeless plain. At one place the road is cut through a hill honeycombed with rock-tombs, which the Haj said were of Jewish origin. Every now and then we passed a *tell*, or great hemispherical mound built up of the rubbish of dozens of ruined towns which, one after the other, were built upon the same site. Even as late as Roman times, this was a densely populated and prosperous district. There is now no timber available for building purposes, and so in a number of villages the houses are constructed with conical roofs of stone. Where the rock happens to be of a reddish tinge, the windowless structures remind one of nothing so much as a collection of Indian wigwams; where the stone is white, as at Tell Biseh, it glitters and sparkles like a city cut out of loaf sugar.

"Hamath the Great," as the prophet Amos called it, is still the most important city between Damascus and Aleppo. It is larger than Homs and seems more prosperous, but the difference between the two is not marked enough to prevent considerable mutual jealousy. Hama is especially busy in the early morning, when the market squares are crowded with kneeling camels and the bazaars are bright with newly opened rolls of rich silks, which may be bought at ridiculously low prices — if the purchaser knows how to bargain.

You see the same types in other Syrian cities — rough camel-drivers, veiled ladies, ragged peasants, underfed soldiers, Moslem wise men and reverend Arab sheikhs. Along tourist-beaten routes, however, the picture lacks somewhat of perfection because of the Hotel d'Orient or Hotel Victoria in the background, and, just as you have warmed to an enthusiastic interest in the bright scenes of Oriental life, a pert young fellow in French clothes is apt to ask you into his shop or offer to guide you through the bazaars at ten francs a day. But while we were in Hama there was, so far as I know, no other Frank in the city, only one other pair of European trousers, and but two natives who spoke any English. There is not even a resident missionary, and on the rare occasions when American ladies visit the city, they adopt the local costume, veil and all, in order to avoid annoying curiosity.

The citizens enjoyed us fully as much as we did them. Everywhere we went we were followed by a train of a dozen or two, and when we stopped to look at anything the crowd threatened to interfere with traffic — not that this would have seemed a serious offense to the Oriental mind! They were so interested in our every movement that I could never get room to use my camera until my friend would walk a little way off with an intense expression on his face and draw the cortège after him. Yet these people were not in the least noisy or rude and — I almost hesitate to make such a startling statement about a Syrian city — I do not remember being once asked for *bakhsheesh*.

The inhabitants of Hama bear the reputation of being very proud and fanatical; but we did not find them so. We stayed with a young physician, a recent graduate of the college at Beirut; and in the evening a number of his friends dropped in to see us. As our own supply of Arabic was not at that time equal to the demands of a long conversation, we essayed one or two gymnastic tricks, only to be immediately outdone by our Syrian acquaintances. Then the ice was broken, and we settled down to a long evening of rough games, which always ended in somebody having his hand slapped with a knotted handkerchief. These strangely garbed men with their brown, wrinkled faces, entered into it all with such a childlike enjoyment that we were soon laughing and shouting as we had not done since the Christmas days of boyhood; and the little brazier, with its bright bed of charcoal that sent fearsome shadows of turbaned heads and long mustachios dancing on the white walls overhead, seemed a natural substitute for the Yule log which that very night was burning in the home across the seas.

As the Christians form a quite insignificant minority of the population of Hama, they receive a degree of consideration from their Moslem neighbors such as is not granted in cities where the two religions are more nearly balanced and where jealousy and hatred consequently lead to frequent reprisals. Our host, Dr. Taufik, told us that some of his warmest friends were young Moslems. He has a large practice among the harems of the city, and has performed heroic operations upon their inmates. One afternoon he guided us through a narrow, winding lane filled with evil-smelling garbage, to a rude door not over five feet high. This was the entrance to the finest house in Hama, the residence of one of the doctor's Moslem patients. Indeed, Dr. Taufik told us, with perhaps more of civic pride than strict accuracy, that it was the most magnificent dwelling in all Syria. The great central hall was decorated in mosaics of colored marble and overlaid with gold-leaf in intricate patterns of sumptuous beauty. Yet, as is so often the case in the East, the only approach to this splendid residence was through filth and odors which would hardly have been tolerated in the worst slums of an American city.

We later visited the home of another wealthy Moslem, also a patient of the doctor. This time we found the master of the house seated in the middle of the state drawing-room — being shaved. He is the only man I have ever seen who looked dignified while in the hands of a barber. Even with lather all over his face, he sat with the bearing of a prince of the blood giving audience to his favorites. His attitude toward us was marked by the most kindly courtesy. He allowed us to indulge in the untidy American habit of wearing shoes in the house, and, although it was the fast-month of Ramadan and he himself could eat nothing until sunset, delicious sweetmeats were served us in delicate cut-glass dishes set on a heavy silver tray. After we had watched our host put on his furs and drive off behind his two beautiful Arab stallions, we asked Dr. Taufik how much wealth was necessary for one to live in such luxury, and what was the business of his Moslem friend. "Oh, he does not work at all," was the answer. "He does not need to, for he has property which brings him an income of forty thousand piasters a year"— which equals a little over fourteen hundred dollars!

Hama has an acropolis somewhat larger than that of Homs, but it is less symmetrical in shape and is not so well preserved. From the summit is seen the same far-reaching historic plain; but the attention is soon drawn back to the city which lies just below. If the visitor has resided in Syria, it is not the twenty-four minarets which hold his gaze, not even the Great Mosque, which is one of many shrines that claim to guard the bones of John the Baptist; but beautiful and interesting above all is the river which winds its slender cord of blue through the heart of the city. Rising on the eastern slopes of Lebanon, then passing northward through Hollow Syria and the Entering In of Hamath, dammed up by the old Hittites to form the Holy Lake by Homs, growing slowly as it flows through the "Land of Hama" until at Antioch it is almost deep enough for modern shipping — the Orontes fathered three of the great cities of the ancient world.

There are few real rivers in this land. Although they make Damascus so fertile, Abana and Pharpar are hardly more than noisy creeks. It is true that parts of Lebanon fairly sweat with springs, but hardly half a dozen of these reach the coast except as winter torrents whose stony beds dry up completely when the summer comes. The Jordan in the far south, the Leontes, which flows into the Mediterranean between Tyre and Sidon, and the Orontes in the north — these complete the tale of Syrian rivers, and Hama is the only city in the country whose stream appears as a prominent feature in the landscape. It winds and twists so that you meet it at almost every turn of the street. Along one bank, a line of closely latticed windows mark the harems of the wealthier citizens; farther on, a little group of women are washing clothes under the shade of the cypress trees; yonder a weary train of mules are standing knee-deep in the cool water, while a crowd of naked boys are sporting in the shallow stream with as much energy and enjoyment as any truant brothers of the West.

It is perhaps because the Orontes goes to the northward instead of flowing south, as do the other important Syrian rivers, that it is now known as *el-'Asi*, "the Rebel"; or the name may have been given, as some old Moslem writers suggest, because its channel is so low that the stream cannot be used for irrigation unless its water is artificially raised.

There is a noise so loud and constant that you have almost ceased to hear it — a dull, grave diapason, fuller and deeper than the heaviest organ-stop. Now, slowly and painfully, it forces up a few tones of the scale, then drops sullenly to its key-note. "Do mi sol, DO DO DO. Do sol la, DO DO DO"— on through the day and the night and the century. It is the music of the *na'ûra*, the water-wheels of the Orontes. You see them now and then in southern villages, but as other cataracts are to Niagara, so are all other water-wheels to the water-wheels of Hama. Great wooden frames revolving painfully upon wooden axles as, by means of buckets along the circumference, the river lifts itself up to the level of the terraces above — these wheels approach very near to perpetual motion. We stand amazed before one that is forty feet high, until the eye travels down the river to another wheel of sixty feet; and our guide takes us out to the edge of the city where a monster ninety feet in diameter is playing its slow, solemn tune.

It is impossible to shut out the sound of their creaking. I know of travelers who have been so distracted by the incessant, inescapable noise that they could not sleep in Hama; but we found the music of the wheels very soothing, like the distant roar of the ocean or a slow fugue played on some cyclopean organ. Now they are in unison, now repeating the theme one after another, now for a brief moment in a sublime harmony never to be forgotten, then once more together in the unison of a tremendous chorus.

As we drift to sleep, the song of the river calls us back, back, back to the Beginning of Things.

"Do mi fa, DO DO DO." What care the wheels whether Saracen or Crusader conquer in the fight below! "Do fa sol, DO DO DO." The chariots of Zenobia are rattling across the plain — or is it the fleeing cohorts of the Assyrian host? "Do sol la, DO DO DO." The dark regiments of Pharaoh are coming up from the south, and the Hittite city rushes to arms. "Do mi sol, DO DO *do* do." And old Orontes is slowly pushing around the great wheels of the dream city, while the Iliad is unsung, and Cheops is unquarried, and the fathers of Abram still dwell in Ur of the Chaldees.

INDEX

INDEX

Roman numerals refer to chapters, Arabic to pages

INDEX

INDEX

INDEX

INDEX

Made in the USA
Charleston, SC
22 February 2014